# COME TO THE WATERS

*Baptism and Our Ministry
of
Welcoming Seekers and Making Disciples*

DANIEL T. BENEDICT, JR.

DISCIPLESHIP RESOURCES
MATERIALS FOR GROWTH IN CHRISTIAN FAITH & LIFE
— NASHVILLE, TENNESSEE —
P.O. Box 840 • Nashville, TN 37202-0840

Library of Congress Catalog Card No. 96-86607

ISBN 0-88177-179-1

DR179

Ho, everyone who thirsts,
    come to the waters;
and you that have no money
    come, buy and eat!
Come, buy wine and milk
    without money and without price.
Why do you spend your money for that which is not bread,
    and your labor for that which does not satisfy?
Listen carefully to me, and eat what is good,
    and delight yourselves in rich food.
Incline your ear, and come to me;
    listen so that you may live.
I will make with you an everlasting covenant,
    my steadfast, sure love for David.

Isaiah 55:1-3

# Abbreviations and Notes to Readers

UMH        *The United Methodist Hymnal*
(sometimes referred to as the Hymnal)

UMBOW     *The United Methodist Book of Worship*
(sometimes referred to as the Book of Worship)
Note: items in UMBOW are numbered in sequence, so references to them are by number and by page (p. ).

Words in italics, except when used for emphasis, indicate that a definition of the word can be found in the Word List at the end of this book.

# CONTENTS

# PREFACE

One night long ago, three riders were traveling across a desert. As they crossed the dry bed of a river, out of the darkness a voice called, "Halt!" They obeyed. The voice told them to dismount, to pick up some pebbles, to put them in their pockets, and to remount. The voice then said, "You have done as I commanded. Tomorrow at sunup you will be both glad and sorry." Mystified, the riders rode on. When the sun rose, they reached into their pockets and found that a miracle had happened. The pebbles had been transformed into diamonds. They remembered the warning. They were both glad and sorry—glad they had taken some, and sorry they had not taken more.[1]

This book invites you and other leaders in your congregation to stop on your journey, to dismount, and to pick up some strangely familiar things. My hope is that with the illumination of the Spirit, you may discover that you have diamonds in your hands. Ordinary stones can become valuable stepping stones to a new way of understanding, leading, and being congregations. This will not happen without transformation, but it can happen if you are willing to face resistance—inward and outward—and are willing to be excited and surprised by grace. As you read and reflect, you will likely encounter your own resistance and surprise—resistance because there are old things here that have been discarded and shelved as no longer useful, excitement and surprise because the realities of our emerging cultural context are casting new light on what is central and basic to being a Christian community on the edge of a new millennium.

This book invites you to entertain a way of congregational life that sends down new and deeper roots into the bedrock of Christian tradition and to begin living intentionally as a missionary people in a culture that is increasingly unchurched. The task of leading the congregation today is complex and difficult. North Americans range from indifference to hostility in their attitudes toward the church. Churches and their leaders feel increasingly sidelined and ignored in our culture. Many congregations feel the pinch of having their backs against the wall financially. The quest to survive saps the energy and vision of leaders and people alike. Just keeping the church doors open hinders us from following Jesus in listening to people who are searching for God. The response is often to try harder and harder by doing the same things we have been doing: more activities, more programs, more accommodation to the culture's values and preferences. We keep trying to do more with less, and the results seem meager.

At the same time that our congregations are experiencing discouragement with the results of their efforts, there is an unprecedented wave of spiritual hunger in our culture. People are looking for meaning, love, and belonging wherever there is promise of spiritual reality. Look at the books people are reading, the movies and television shows they are watching, the proliferation of recovery groups and new age movements they are joining. Why do adults turn to these resources as diamonds and pass by our congregations as if they were piles of worthless stones?

Perhaps many congregations are preoccupied with the church, while the risen

Lord has moved ahead of us to care about people who are looking for God. Could it be that we ourselves are being called to lives of fresh discipleship and attentiveness to the means of grace? Could it be that Jesus is calling you and your faith community to discover that the seemingly worthless pebbles that have been tossed onto the rock pile of religious artifacts are in reality diamonds for searching adults and youth? What if the classical means of grace—prayer, searching the Scriptures, listening to God, sharing the stories of daily life and work, and struggling to love God and our neighbor—prove to be the ways to spiritual vitality and healing for seekers and believers alike? What if our treasured words and sacraments were accompanied by deeds of mercy and power? What wondrous things might happen as people journey in the desert before sunup?

This book is about a way of welcoming people as they are, listening to their stories and questions, mentoring them as they listen to God, forming and initiating them into a life of discipleship by using the means of grace, and commissioning them to live lives of continuing conversion and service to God in their daily relationships.

This book is written for pastors and other congregational leaders who care about and prayerfully lead the people of God. While it is written specifically for United Methodist leaders, I hope that leaders in other traditions will find the book provocative and applicable. This is not a program or a prescription to plug in like an appliance you buy at a discount store. That approach will end with nothing but another stone to cast aside. If, however, you will listen and stay open to the Spirit who has power to put flesh and skin on these bones and to breathe life into them, then you will be surprised at the transformation that takes place. What happened in the valley of dry bones (Ezekial 37), can become the story of what happens to you and your people as you journey with those God is calling to be Christ's disciples.

I am grateful to all who have encouraged, guided, challenged, and dreamed with me in birthing this book: Hoyt Hickman, Alan Detscher, Joseph Russell, and Karen Ward at Consultation on Common Texts meetings; my colleagues at the General Board of Discipleship, especially Ezra Earl Jones, whose thinking always goads me to turn stones and to see them in a new light; Grant Sperry White, Karen Westerfield Tucker, and William McDonald, who have gazed with me at stones from the past and joined in the task of unearthing them for use in resources today; generous mentors in the Episcopal and Evangelical Lutheran Churches who have welcomed me to their times of learning and simulation of Christian initiation; Robert Webber whose evangelical and catholic passions prompt me to repent of ever separating the two; real people like Jeremy and Laura whose quest for God from atheistic beginnings grounded this book in real life stories; Mary Alice McKinney who dreamed and encouraged me to write; Craig Gallaway who prodded me to go deeper; Barbara Bate and Anne Burnette Hook who rejoiced whenever the tiger got out of the cage; the staff of Discipleship Resources whose patience and publishing knowledge move ideas in the head to resources in print; Joane Pettus who used her spiritual gift of helping to care for many details and freed me to write; and Mary O. Benedict who lives and prays with me, and who, a long time ago, modeled for me what it means to support someone on a conversion journey. For all of these people, *Deo gratia*.

—Daniel T. Benedict, Jr.

# INTRODUCTION

The chair of a congregation's board of trustees was asked why the church had not made its buildings accessible to persons with handicapping conditions. The trustee answered, "There was no need to make them accessible; we have no handicapped people." The insensitivity of the response is tragic and unworthy of the gospel of Jesus Christ. Think of the story as a parable of the present-day need for accessibility to life in Christ for people who are seeking God. Many congregations of the mainline variety do not have adequate structures or processes in place for persons who are searching for God. Though no one would actually say it, the present reality of many congregations today shouts, "Why would we need to have a process in place for making faith more accessible? We don't have unconverted people coming to us." We are asleep in the light.

Institutionalized Christianity is much like many of our old church buildings. You have to walk *up* ten steps to get into the sanctuary or *down* four steps to get into the social hall. In short they are inaccessible for many people. People without background in modern church life with its complex programs and organization, formal style, assumption of biblical knowledge, and unfamiliar musical idioms are effectively kept out of the community of faith.

Facing this reality about your congregation is essential. If your congregation is not reaching new people with the good news of Jesus Christ, receiving them into the fellowship of the church, nurturing them in discipleship, and helping them find their own place of creative service in the world, then it is in fact missing its primary and essential work.[2] Many congregations are in danger of ceasing to be what they are truly called to be.

The good news is that the ministry of your congregation and your life together can be different. God can use you in a new way to make the good news of Jesus Christ accessible to people seeking God. The purpose of this book is to describe and explore a process for doing evangelism, formation in discipleship, and initiation into the community of faith so that your congregation serves people who are searching for love, belonging, faith, and hope.

## REDISCOVERING THE WAY OF ACCESSIBILITY

The source of the process that we will be exploring in this book may be surprising to United Methodists, with our early Anglican roots and our colorful American frontier experience. We might think that the source is to be found in the writings of John Wesley or in the camp meeting stories and the lore of the circuit riders' resourceful efforts. Indeed, a similar kind of accessibility is found there; but the source is much earlier than those chapters of church history, which straddle the Atlantic Ocean of the eighteenth and nineteenth centuries.

The clock has to be turned back at least to events described in the Book of Acts and to the 250 years that followed them. The map we need is not of Northern Europe or North America but of the ancient world of the Fertile Crescent and the

Mediterranean Sea and places like Jerusalem, Syria, Rome, and Carthage.[3]

In Acts 8 we read of an encounter that took place on the road from Jerusalem to Gaza and contained the elements of the process we will call *Christian initiation*. An Ethiopian eunuch was heading south on his way home from Jerusalem. He was engaged in reading Isaiah. Philip, prompted by the Spirit, went to him and asked if he understood what he was reading. "How can I, unless someone guides me?" the eunuch answered (Acts 8:31).

He invited Philip to get into the chariot with him and a relationship began to form around his quest and questions. The miles passed under the chariot while Philip proclaimed the good news of Jesus Christ. With water in sight, the Ethiopian asked Philip if there was any reason that would stop him from being baptized. This may have been a question about whether or not there was a social barrier to prevent his being baptized because he was a eunuch. (Philip knew there was no barrier to anyone coming in faith.)

The journey then moved into the water of baptism. After the baptism, Philip was spirited away to other towns and the eunuch went his way rejoicing. Whoosh! It all happened so fast. It seemed so simple. But what can we learn from this about baptism and Christian initiation today?

The important thing for our purposes is not the sudden and dramatic, but the sequence of events and the elements that make up the logic of the conversion process.

- **Search**: a person's quest, a person's inquiry about God;

- **Discipleship**: a believer, yielding to the promptings of the Spirit to reach out and, listen to seekers;

- **Journey**: two persons' reflecting with each other on the Scriptures and proclamation of the good news of Jesus;

- **Discernment**: a mutual sense of readiness to respond to Jesus and the good news;

- **Initiation**: the faith community's baptizing a person into a life of faith in Jesus Christ;

- **Joy and Transformation**: the power and reality of conversion and initiation, bringing joy and transformation of life.

The sequence and elements of this story and others in the Book of Acts illustrate the logic and flow of evangelization, conversion, formation, and initiation that developed in the early centuries of the church. As we shall see, this same sequence appears in the pattern of Christian initiation that developed in the church during the third and fourth centuries.

## THE SHAPE OF EVANGELISM, FORMATION, AND CHRISTIAN INITIATION IN THE EARLY CHURCH[4]

Now turn the clock forward two centuries. Early Christian communities, in their ministry and witness in daily life, attracted others who inquired about the hope in Jesus Christ and about being his followers. The believers so identified with ordinary people that some of the seekers experienced the presence of Jesus listening to and caring for them in their struggles and cares. A journey was begun, questions were asked, stories of pilgrimage were told (both by the inquirers and the believers), the reality of Jesus was shared, relationships were formed, and faith grew. Do you recognize the pattern?

When their questions had been wrestled with sufficiently and there came a mutual discernment of readiness to enter into a life with the Christians, the inquirers were welcomed as catechumens or "hearers." *Catechumen* comes from the Greek word for "sound in the ear." The *catechumens* were hearers because the church invited them to hear the Word of God with the community of faith and to learn the Christian way of life. Sponsors walked with the hearers as they made their journey toward the waters of baptism.

As conversion and growth took place in the hearers, the journey was marked by a decision to be baptized. They were called to baptism, and their names were written in a large book as candidates for baptism. The community of faith invited them to share their life of worship, prayer, belief, and service. Together, they engaged in intense reflection on the lectionary texts read and preached during the services of worship. The pilgrims were invited to pray and meditate on the Word, with their sponsors and the congregation, as they prepared for entrance into the good news of Christ's victory over sin and death. Special leaders called *catechists* gave guidance and teaching. The sponsors were ever present to the candidates as spiritual friends and guides.

The intense period of preparation for baptism occurred in the days just before Easter. If the candidates were ready, they shared a vigil of fasting, prayer, and an examination of conscience. As the sponsors had been with them all along the journey, they now led them to the pool where they were baptized at the vigil before Easter. There, on the night commemorating the Lord's rising, they were initiated into the faith of the community through baptism, laying on of hands, and the Eucharist.

But this was not the end of the journey! The Christian community knew that the process did not end with the high point of baptism, laying on of hands, and the Lord's Supper. Opportunity to explore this mystery with reflection was called *mystagogia*—instruction and reflection on the mystery of salvation, the sacraments, and participation in the ministry of the church. During the weeks between Easter and Pentecost, the church helped the newly baptized (*neophytes*) to make sense of the intense and transforming experience they had had. No longer candidates, they stood within the community to view the sacraments of baptism and the Eucharist as the Word present among them. Now they had been fully initiated into Christ's converted and converting people. Now the living Lord would lead them as his disciples and they would represent him in the world through daily-life ministry.[5]

The rest of their lives would be lived out in a new vocation in common with other Christians. In them the flow of grace in and through the church had come full circle, and the witness of the faith community was expanded through the church into the world. Women and men and families were drawn to the good news of Jesus Christ. The whole congregation was energized by and organized around the flow of God's grace in initiating persons into the life of faith.

The process was ongoing. Outreach, open dialogue, caring relationships, ministry and faith continuously expanded the circle that took in more and more persons. The faithful, rooted in the baptismal covenant that God had made with them, carried on the essential ministry that had started them on their journey.

Our context today is different, but the process of forming Christians invites the same engagement with people on a journey of faith and experience through worship, prayer, Scripture, and service. The essential ministry of reaching, receiving, discipling, and sending, remains the same. The essence of the invitation is the same: Come share the journey with us. Come follow Jesus with us. Come to the waters of belonging to him.

## CHRISTIAN INITIATION AND THE CONGREGATION

Today, when a congregation celebrates the service of the baptismal covenant[6], the welcome and vows of the congregation presume a community that has the faith, will, readiness, and ability to welcome, pray for, surround, mentor, and share in ministry with others. The goal of all is that "in everything God may be glorified through Jesus Christ" (UMH, 38). The members of the congregation not only reaffirm their rejection of sin and commitment to Christ but also promise to include the candidates in their care, saying:

> **With God's help we will proclaim the good news**
> **and live according to the example of Christ.**
> **We will surround *these persons***
> **with a community of love and forgiveness,**
> **that *they* may grow in *their* trust of God,**
> **and be found faithful in *their* service to others.**
> **We will pray for *them*,**
> **that *they* may be true disciples**
> **who walk in the way that leads to life.[7]**

These are weighty promises. They are promises to include the newly incorporated and to share with them in a common journey and a common life of faith. How can Christians promise so much and expect the candidates to enter such a covenant? How indeed? How can we, unless the transforming grace of God has been at work and there is *already* a sense of relationship and care? We can promise a covenant community if we can begin by saying, "We know these people. We have heard their story and watched their lives changed in worship, prayer, Bible study, and service. God has tested our love for them and their love for us! We welcome them into Christ's royal priesthood. Thanks be to God!"

In other words, the promises the congregation makes at the baptism of new believers can only be meaningful and trustworthy when our congregation as a whole is already fulfilling its essential ministry. The reason is simple: The services of the baptismal covenant assume that there is a nurturing, disciple-making community leading persons toward the waters of baptism and baptismal faith and the same community will continue the process of nurture and mutual ministry subsequent to Holy Baptism.

When the congregation addresses the newly initiated, the words can only have integrity and depth if those persons have been reached out to, welcomed, nurtured, and affirmed by the community as a whole. The role that Philip played in reaching out to the Ethiopian eunuch belongs to the whole congregation. That, in turn, requires deliberate and prayerful formation of the congregation's life and vision.

Thus—and this is crucial—Christian initiation has to do with the shape and formation of the whole congregation's life in fulfilling its essential ministry. The congregation must become a welcoming, forming, and sending community in its ongoing worship, reflection, prayer, and ministry.

## A FOCUS ON THE FLOW OF GRACE

All of this is to say that the full range of congregational life comes into play in fulfilling its disciple-making task. As we have seen, the basic pattern of ministry in Acts 8, in the early church's *catechumenate,* and in our growing understanding of the congregation's essential ministry depends upon and reflects the flow of God's grace through Jesus Christ to the world. In order to sum up this total pattern of welcoming, forming, baptizing, supporting, and sending, we will often use the word *flow* to refer to the movement of God's grace.

In this regard, then, *flow* refers to the transforming power of the gospel embodied in the life of the congregation as it gives itself to Christ for the life of the world. Of course, the flow of God's grace can never be contained or limited to the work of grace in the local church or even in the church universal. God's grace is universally at work in the life of every person and in creation itself. This reality supports the possibility of Christian evangelism and ministry in daily life.

Still, there is a critical need for each congregation to recover a clear and deep sense of the sweep and dynamism of God's mission. For too long North American churches have been fixed on static structures, programs, and activities without this deep sense of participation in what God is doing. The vital understanding that baptism is every Christian's entrance into ministry has atrophied. We have allowed ministry to be seen as what the ordained and Christian professionals do. The work of all of the baptized has shriveled from a powerful, apostolic movement to a tame, religious consumerism. Church life in many congregations relies on specialists or professional leaders, using glossy resources produced by denominational publishing houses. However, the truth remains that the flow of God's grace can never be shrink-wrapped for institutional ends. God is calling your congregation to recover a sense of participation in God's mission through the church for the sake of people who long to know God in Christ.

God's initiative, working in and with faithful disciples, is the vision at the heart of this book. This vision draws the congregation out into the world where real people—hurting people, seeking people—live. This vision calls Christians to embody the good news of Jesus by living among ordinary people and listening to their deepest longings for God. The ministry of Jesus through the disciples can never be complete within the walls of the church building. On this side of the new heaven and the new earth, the nurture and building up of the people of God is never an end in itself.

The risen Lord is working in the lives and experiences of persons, like the Ethiopian eunuch, who are puzzled and searching. Ministry that is conscious of the flow of God's grace moves in the confidence that Jesus Christ lives and goes before us as we listen to and care for people in their hurts and yearnings.

## AN INVITATION AND A RESOURCE

*Come to the Waters* is an invitation to you and your congregation to make the transforming power of God in Christ accessible to all persons, especially those we are least prepared to welcome and form in faith. This resource is designed to accomplish four things:

1. To ground your congregation's ministry in the services of the baptismal covenant by outlining and exploring a process of Christian initiation that comes from the early church.

2. To identify resources and roles that will enable your congregation to establish a flow of evangelism, formation, and initiation, and to welcome and walk with people on their conversion journey.

3. To offer model services and prayers, with introduction and commentary for initiating adults on a journey of conversion that leads to baptism and full participation in the life of discipleship.

4. To provide additional services and prayers with introduction and commentary that enable the process to be adapted for use with persons who seek to affirm their baptism, and with families who desire to present for baptism infants, children, or other persons who cannot answer for themselves.

How can the church gracefully introduce people to the grace-full life? That is the concern of this book. Part One will focus on an approach to welcoming and walking with persons on the journey of conversion. Part Two will provide model services with introduction and commentary that congregations may use in celebrating the stages and transitions of this journey.

# Chapter One

# ADULT CONVERSION
# AND THE EMERGING MISSION FRONTIER

An associate pastor leading in the reception of members in a large, mid-American congregation announced, "Among those we will receive as members today, we have four adults who have never professed the Christian faith. It is unusual to have this many!" The group of adults to be received numbered nearly twenty and most were transfers from other denominations. The pastor's comment symbolized where we North American mainline Protestants are as we stand on the edge of a new millennium. We are surprised by adult conversion and baptism. We have grown accustomed to looking at youth and adults as already baptized, culturally Christian, and ready to join the church of their choice. The grounds for such thinking are rapidly eroding.

The good-old-days culture that we knew in the years 1950-1965, with its slogan *Attend the church of your choice*, is extinct. Religious pluralism used to mean Baptists, Methodists, and Roman Catholics. Now it means Islam, Judaism, Christianity, Buddhism, and a host of other distinctly different spiritual traditions. Increasing numbers of persons have little or no experience of the gospel or of the community of faith gathered around Jesus Christ. We can no longer assume that North Americans are Christian simply because they live in Canada or the United States.

In a diverse and rapidly changing world, there is a new urgency to attend to the congregation's essential work: reaching out to people, welcoming them to the life of faith, forming them as disciples in a covenant community, and commissioning them to love God and neighbor in the world. How persons come to belong and participate in the Christian community needs fresh understanding and bold leadership. Pastors and laity are sensing the necessity of being about the central task to which Jesus calls the church as a living body. The processes and functions of congregational life must recover and embody Jesus' regard for people—people destined for God's reign—if the congregation is to be faithful and fruitful in our time. The urgent need for genuine leadership does not allow aimlessness, business as usual, and ease with the *status quo*. This urgency does not allow leaders to treat the congregation as an end in itself. God's mission will not let us think that small. The reign of God is much larger than your congregation, your denomination, or even the church universal.

## THE EMERGING MISSION FRONTIER

Loren Mead, in his book *The Once and Future Church,* claims that the boundary between world and congregation has become more significant now than at any time in the last 1600 years. The mission frontier is no longer *at the edge* of the culture. It has moved closer to the threshold of the congregation as Christians live in the midst of a "foreign land." Mead calls for a reinvention of the congregation which "has lost some of its capacity to be a reliable ground for initiating, educating, and nurturing each person in faith."[8]

Congregations can no longer assume that the culture has engaged people in any significant contact with Christian tradition. More and more persons are starting from ground zero as they search for the meaning, love, and belonging that prompts them to start out on a journey of seeking God and conversion. They come to churches with little, if any, previous experience with a Christian group or tradition. The environment in which the baby-boomer generation and even younger folk have been formed is culturally more distant from the stories and images of the faith than previous generations born in the twentieth century.

## CONVERSION AND THE CULTURALLY DISTANT

Since ministry reaches *outside* the church, your congregation and its leaders must expand their horizons to ask about the connections between the life of the congregation and God's mission for the life of the world. In our changing culture, the risen Lord is calling your congregation to address the full scope of its essential ministry: sending disciples out that they might *reach* and *receive* others and invite them to share the journey of conversion that is at the core of walking with Jesus.

A majority of mainline Protestant congregations report no adult baptisms and few professions of faith. As in the story of the trustee who asked, "Why do we need to make our building accessible to persons with handicapping conditions?" it is all too easy for congregations to believe and act in ways that say, "We don't have unconverted, unbaptized adults. Why would we need to have a process in place for them?" That response could mean that many, if not most, mainline congregations are organized and operating without an expectation of adult conversion. It also suggests that they are operating with the tacit expectation of extinction by around 2010, especially in view of the percentage of church members who are over sixty-five years of age.

Many, if not most, of our congregations are inadequately prepared to welcome strangers and seekers to the life of faith and love. Many congregations and their leaders assume that the culture is essentially Christian and that most persons are more or less ready to be inducted into membership following a simple orientation to church organization and beliefs. We may hold a parallel assumption that most youth and adults are already members of some denomination (or have been) so that all we need to do is to transfer their membership and to welcome them.

We could be lulled to sleep with these assumptions, if it were not for the uneasy feelings that nag at us. Many who have participated in the reception of members by profession of faith in Christ, by reaffirmation of faith, or by adult baptism recall an uneasy feeling that something is amiss; that the words and actions are not congruent with the experience of the candidate or of the congregation. On such occasions we ask the candidates to promise more than we have prepared them to understand or intend. Imagine: The candidate promises to renounce the spiritual forces of wickedness; to reject evil, injustice, and oppression; to confess Jesus Christ as Savior; wholly trust his grace; to serve him as Lord in union with the church; to declare the authority of the Bible; and to pledge to be loyal to the denomination and the ministries of the local congregation. He or she promises all of this in the span of about two minutes in front of a congregation to whom the candidate is more than likely a stranger!

Similarly, the congregation makes promises to "surround these persons with a community of love and forgiveness that they may grow in their trust of God." Further, the congregation promises to "pray for them, that they may be true disciples." Often the congregation has not seen or met these persons before, let alone surrounded them and prayed for them. (See *UMH*, p. 35, No. 8.)

## TAKING ADULT CONVERSION SERIOUSLY

In light of the emerging mission frontier and the general lack of preparation for its challenges in most congregations, this resource invites you and your congregation to focus on the paradigm of adult conversion. Mission can no longer be paid for at the distant edges of our culture. North American culture is less and less the base of mission outreach to other nations and cultures. *North American culture itself is increasingly a mission field made up of those who are either uninformed, untrained, indifferent, or even hostile to the values and the gospel that the church has pledged itself to embrace and proclaim.*[9]

As we approach a new millennium, the emerging mission frontier is more like that encountered in the first three centuries of the church. The missional paradigm of those early centuries was conversion of adults who were preparing for baptism. This conversion process took as long as three years, because congregations understood that major transformations were necessary in the lives of inquirers. Inquirers' occupations and ways of life were scrutinized, even changed. During the process these men and women

- encountered the good news of Jesus and explored their desire to know it more fully;
- inquired about the journey of conversion;
- received guidance and formation in the way of faith and discipleship;
- reached a mature and mutual decision to be baptized;
- passed through a time of intensive preparation;
- received baptism as the rite of initiation into the people of God and life in the Spirit;
- were integrated into the life and ministry of the church.

*A central conviction of this resource is that the time has come once again to take seriously these basic steps in the pattern of adult conversion and to discover what this could mean for real people living on the emerging mission frontier.*

Who are these persons for whom your congregation must be ready? What are they seeking? What are their needs? What would it look like if the grace of God, embodied in the life your congregation, were working in the lives of adult seekers?

## JEREMY

Consider the case of Jeremy. He grew up in a home that was overtly and unapologetically atheist. In adult life, Jeremy became a broadcast journalist. He was thoughtful, urbane, skeptical.

At forty-something, in a second marriage and settling in Southern California, he attended a service of Christian worship for the first time in his life. He had come because of his teenage son who was visiting for the summer. The son, who lived in Ohio with his mother during the school year, had become an active participant in a church there. Jeremy's June visit to the church was an accommodation to the son's desire to be in worship and in a youth group during the summer he was to spend in California.

The worship service that Jeremy and his family attended happened to be on a Sunday when the pastors were away at annual conference. The worship services that day were led by a team of church members. During the service, an elementary school teacher talked about her faith in an engaging way and Jeremy found himself strangely drawn to the reality of her witness. He heard something that he did not understand, but it stirred his mind and heart.

He came back the next week. People reached out to him and to his spouse and son. The experience was foreign to him. It was, at once, attractive and disconcerting. Jeremy took the initiative to ask questions, express interest, and offer his confusion. He apologized for all he did not know or comprehend.

Ironically, it was the congregation and the leaders who should have been making the apologies and confessing their lack of expectation and preparation for persons beginning their conversion journey in adult life. Jeremy's eagerness to explore the life of faith called for a search at a level deeper and more arduous than the typical membership class the church offered.

Both pastors welcomed Jeremy's inquiries and searchings. They met with him as he expressed his need for understanding and meaning. Leaders and congregation were unprepared for a serious seeker who did not have through infant baptism even a nominal status as a Christian. This is not to diminish the sacrament of baptism at any age. Tragically, however, many infant baptisms are little more than nominal because congregations and leaders have not accompanied baptized children and their families on the journey of prayer and caring reflection that leads to mature discipleship.

On All Saints Day of 1992, five months later, Jeremy was baptized. He had taken a journey. In many ways the congregation gave Jeremy inadequate support. Jeremy was not sure if he was ready. The pastors were likewise uncertain. Despite these reservations, however, he entered the baptismal waters and the community of faith. Some significant growth had taken place. He had experienced in powerful ways the Word of God in worship, sermon, and faith community. A loving couple had graciously enacted and personalized the congregation's care for Jeremy, though no one had formally asked them to do so.

How could this congregation and its leaders have better helped Jeremy? How could the congregation have better helped Jeremy make the journey to faith and to baptism and, through baptism, to full Christian discipleship? What if Jeremy had taken the journey of conversion in the company of a congregation that gave intentional structure and nurture to the full range of his inner searchings and questions? What if the congregation had been ready to journey with Jeremy in its life of worship, prayer, Bible study, and ministry? What if the congregation had been prepared for an adult inquirer in such a way that in will, faith, and worship, it could welcome, pray for, surround, mentor, and share in ministry with him both before and after baptism?

## LAURA

Now consider Laura's story. She too was born to a family that had rejected God. Her father grew up in a Roman Catholic family, but he had rejected the church in adult life. Her mother was born in an Episcopalian home, but had left the church in the eighth grade. The particularity of Jesus had been scandalous in her youth and in her family's philosophical discussions. While overtly rejecting Christianity in the context of her parent's rejection, Laura recalls having a spiritual sense in her love of art, music, and nature. She experienced awe in the world of sensing.

In adult life, she was in and out of counseling. During two years of intensive psychotherapy because of severe anxiety, Laura began, in her words, to learn faith in herself. The word *faith* in her working vocabulary led her to consider the possibility of faith in something greater. She said that she found herself having a sense of overwhelming, undefinable gratitude. She experienced a need to go to church to see if there might be something there for her.

She first attended worship during the week before Easter in 1993. As she put it, "It was like taking part in a great dramatic play." She went through Holy Week and Easter. "I am still knocked out by what goes on and the joy of it," she recalled. She asked the rector of this Episcopal church, "How does someone thirty-nine years old and *not baptized* find out about all this?" Ironically, just the week before, the priest and the Christian education director had discussed starting a process for initiation of adults and they had wondered where they would find an adult who had not been baptized.

Laura became part of a group of seven persons who were hearers (*catechumens*) preparing for baptism. She told the priest, "I don't know if I can ever believe all this, but I am drawn to the Eucharist." When asked what was the best part of all of this process, Laura said, "Everyone has problems and questions. This experience allowed me to grow spiritually at my own pace. Seeing how God works through us has given me the greatest encouragement and inspiration." At the Easter Vigil in 1994, Laura was baptized into Christ's royal priesthood and accepted God's grace and claim on her life.

How can our congregations better reach out to people where they are and receive them as they are so that they can journey to where God invites them to be?

In our culture, there are increasing numbers of Jeremys and Lauras who do not have an inner world populated with the stories of Adam and Eve, Moses and Miriam, David and Goliath, Mary and Joseph, Jesus, Mary Magdalene, Paul, Priscilla, and Aquila. For them, cross, grace, Communion, creeds, hymns, and prayer are only words on a page.

There are so many seekers like Jeremy and Laura who have inner stirrings. They know that something strange, odd, inchoate, and nameless is stirring inside them. They know they are searching for a new center of gravity. What are they to do? If God is real, how will they know? Who will see their search with the eyes of both mind and heart? Who will help them? Who will help them name this journey and bring it out into the light? Who in your congregation can identify with their story? Who is prepared to share the faith journey with seekers so that they too can know God and discover eternal life using the means of grace?

Jeremy and Laura might have taken and may still enroll in seminary courses because they have a deep need to grow in understanding and in discipleship. Aidan Kavanagh says that many of his students at Yale were there because the congregations in which they started their conversion journey were not prepared to help them name and make public their inner quest for meaning in the experience of great mystery.[10] What if your congregation became a community of faith with such depth of experience and spiritual guidance that adult seekers found themselves growing at their own pace and being drawn to Christ, who is known in the Word and at the table, served in the ordinary round of daily life, and loved in a continuing process of conversion?

## ADULT SEEKERS, BAPTISM, AND OUR TWENTY-FIRST CENTURY CONTEXT

During the last sixteen hundred years, Western Christianity has relied upon an infant/child baptism model. Relying upon this infant baptism model, congregations have welcomed new persons born into its families. In towns and villages that were perceived as being settled and Christian, the normal process was for families to offer their young children for baptism and the life of faith. The church that most of us know has become accustomed to growth by adding the children of adult members through baptism and subsequent nurture and instruction that lead to some form of adult profession of faith celebrated as confirmation. The heavy emphasis on nurturing the child subsequent to baptism makes good sense when dealing with Christian families who are prepared to raise their children in the church. In the infant baptism model, the progression is baptism followed by nurture, conversion, and profession of faith.

With the rapid emergence of a new mission frontier in North America, missionary congregations must begin to adopt a different model: adult conversion leading to baptism. Rather than the sacrament of baptism followed by nurture, the picture is one of conversion leading to baptism and a continuing journey with other disciples.

The church will continue to baptize infants and to lead youth who have grown up in the church to profess their faith and to be confirmed as Christian disciples. The processes of adult initiation set forth in this book in no way seek to discourage the baptism of the children of believing families. Nevertheless, the shift to a focus on unbaptized adults is crucial if your congregation is to recover the full missionary potential of its essential ministry. *By Water and the Spirit* states:

> Adult baptism is the norm when the Church is in a missionary situation, reaching out to persons in a culture which is indifferent or hostile to the faith. While the baptism of infants is appropriate for Christian families, the increasingly minority status of the Church in contemporary society demands more attention to evangelizing, nurturing, and baptizing adult converts.[11]

Contemporary Christian initiation, based on the early church's pattern of adult conversion and initiation has three stages: evangelization, formation, and initiation. This pattern is not a renouncing of the practice of infant baptism. It is a shift of emphasis in light of the new mission frontier where ever larger numbers of persons have either not been baptized or, though baptized, have not had significant experience and nurture in a Christian community. This shift of focus to adult baptism has precedent in church history whenever the church has been thrust into a clearly missionary context. When the dominant culture does not identify with the Christian faith, the church cannot assume that persons have a background shaped by the stories, images, values, and traditions of the church and the Bible. The faith community must intentionally guide and nurture seekers so that they come to the waters of baptism consciously professing a faith that is relationally rooted in the truth of the gospel and the gospel community.

On the one hand, all persons, adults or children, are born anew from the baptismal waters. All of us come from the font or pool as children of God. Each newborn Christian participates in God's new creation with the developmental capacity that each possesses at his or her stage of life. Stewardship of life and Jesus' way of engaging people where they are in their journey demand nothing less than adequate and attentive guidance, nurture, and attention.

## Infant Baptism Model

Baptism     Nurture     Conversion     Profession of Faith     Discipleship and Ministry

## Adult Baptism Model

Inquiry and Search     Conversion     Formation     Baptism     Discipleship and Ministry

If, on the other hand, we continue to neglect an adult conversion pattern leading to baptism or to profession of faith and reaffirmation of the baptismal covenant, we will prolong two major misunderstandings of baptism: (1) that baptism has little significance in God's gracious ways with people and (2) that baptism magically or irrevocably conveys God's grace. Baptism is neither useless nor magic.[12] Rather, baptism is God's gracious gift at a key moment in the candidate's journey. We will explore baptism in greater depth in Chapter Two.

While baptism is initiatory, taking seriously an adult pattern of conversion means assuming that much will precede and follow it. We must not limit our understanding of baptism to converting grace at a point in time. Indeed, in order to rightly understand converting grace, we must see how it is embedded in God's work of prevenient and convincing grace and how it leads to sanctifying grace. Likewise, the process of Christian initiation is not a form of works righteousness or law. Rather, it aims at embodying the relational and personal way in which the Spirit of Jesus Christ brings people into the community of faith and the reign of God.

The essential ministry of the church has at its core the work of God: drawing persons into the community, welcoming them, forming faith, working in them repentance and conversion, nurturing faith, equipping them, and sending them out to be disciples in the world (see Matthew 28:19-20). The focus on adult conversion and baptism takes seriously the congregation's work in collaboration with God on this real and human journey. One can only imagine the potential of congregations that orient their life and ministry around such a missionary vision.

## A PROCESS FOR THE IN-BETWEEN

As stated above, there are three major movements in the process whereby persons are initiated into the community of faith: (1) evangelization (pre-conversion), (2) formation and instruction (*catechesis*), and (3) the sacrament of initiation itself. There are, of course, other movements or steps that precede and follow these in the total flow of God's grace. Here, however, we will focus on the events surrounding baptism. Think in terms of the structures of a house. The first movement, evangelization, corresponds with the steps; the second, formation and instruction, with the porch; and the third, initiation, with the doorway into the house.

Like some modern homes, many contemporary congregations do not have a porch. People who are searching for God need more than abruptly ascending steps that usher them directly into the house. They are not ready for that. Steps that lead to an open space where they can test, explore, search, and experience God's welcome in the faith community, are analogous to a porch. Porches are gracious spaces between the steps and the house. On a porch, the people who live inside and the people who are approaching can meet, begin to know one another, and experience the climate of the house. A porch is a gracious space, open and hospitable. On the porch there is no rush to relationship or commitment. On a porch there is room to meet, explore, tell stories, and test what these new relationships might mean. On a porch, the congregation can extend the invitation to come inside when it senses that what has been shared on the porch recommends this invitation. Likewise, the seeker can evaluate and discern whether he or she has an interest in fuller participation in the life of the household of faith. A porch is an in-between place for people who are seeking God.

Aidan Kavanagh writes:

> Without *evangelization*, catechesis has nothing to work with, and the rites of initiation in that case can only be dissimulated [concealed under a false appearance]. Without *catechesis*, the initial conversion occasioned by evangelization (which is often deeply subjective, incommunicable, and euphoric) cannot be nurtured, steadied, broadened into a coherent world view and brought to ecclesial term. And without the *sacraments of initiation* [baptism, confirmation, and Eucharist], catechesis loses its primary focus. . . .[13]

The primary question this resource raises is this: *Is your congregation prepared to offer an in-between place to persons whose lives have "been upended by the grace of conversion"?*[14] *Come to the Waters* offers your congregation a vision and a process for creating the crucial middle element to this three-part movement.

Aidan Kavanagh's outline of the threefold movement of evangelization, catechesis, and initiation will help you to diagnose some of the fundamental ailments that afflict your congregation's will and ability to offer a much-needed porch to those who are in between evangelization and initiation.

First, unless we trust and expect God to act in the lives of people who are searching for love, meaning, and belonging, there is little *we* can do that will meet their deepest needs. Any prospect of the congregation's forming people as disciples must be preceded by the gracious and mysterious work of the Holy Spirit in their lives.

Second, if our congregations circumvent the arduous, but essential, work of formation of disciples, the inward, almost private experience of God's prevenient grace will more than likely come to nothing that looks like conversion and consistent Christian living. Our clear apostolic mandate is to make disciples (Matthew 28:18-20).

Third, when instruction and formation are conducted without a primary and defining focus, our human tendency will always be to focus on subjectively selected and parochial norms or to dissipate the focus to a general intention to be good people, in terms that look much like the surrounding culture's measure of good citizens. In contrast to this, when the focus of making disciples is clearly placed upon the baptismal covenant, the congregation and its leaders have a clear basis for what can be expected on the journey of conversion before and after baptism. The baptismal covenant serves as a clear foundation for Christian formation and for lifelong accountability among Christians.

We turn attention to baptism and the congregration's essential ministry in the next chapter.

---

## BASIC CONCEPTS IN CHAPTER ONE

❧ A new mission frontier is emerging on which increasing numbers of adults are culturally distant from the good news of Jesus Christ and the faith of the church.

❧ Faithful response to this emerging mission frontier requires that congregations and their leaders take adult conversion with a fresh seriousness.

❧ Understanding adult conversion as a journey opens the way for the congregation and its leaders to offer seekers a porch for experience, reflection, relationships, and formation in the life of faith and discipleship.

❧ There are three major movements in the process of initiating persons into the community of faith:

1. Evangelization (steps)

2. Formation (porch)

3. Initiation (the door)

Chapter Two

# BAPTISM AND YOUR CONGREGATION'S ESSENTIAL MINISTRY

*"There is a river whose streams make glad the city of God."*
Psalm 46:4a

The church today is like Ponce de Leon, the Spanish explorer, who is reputed to have searched for the fountain of youth. The search is on! Many pastors and leaders are turning to seminars and consultants to find approaches that will help their congregations break out of ways that are not yielding desired results. Church judicatories are talking about new paradigms and there is a growing willingness to leap the fence of conservatism to risk being the church in new ways. Phrases like *entrepreneurial leadership, visionary leadership,* and *spiritual leadership* are in vogue as the church tries to get beyond management of the current reality and to move out of the ecclesiastical doldrums. A number of the mega-churches are becoming teaching churches, offering week-long seminars that promise to turn around aging and declining congregations. All of this says that mainline Protestant congregations are anxious to find the secret of what will rejuvenate their flagging life together. Where does your congregation look for renewal? Where is that place of rejuvenation and life? Could it be that in the church the primal spring is so close that it is overlooked?

## THE SPRING OF BAPTISM

On the farm where I lived as a young boy, there was a spring on a nearby hill. It supplied our house and barn with cool, satisfying water. I remember being fascinated with the spring, in part because it was home to a rainbow trout that someone had placed there. The spring was protected by a cement casing with a cover on it. From sources deep in the ground the water rose up to supply all who would drink. The sources were hidden, but the water was real and satisfying.

Without that spring, our farm would have been uninhabitable. In day-to-day life, we turned on the faucet and drank and bathed. We did not worry about the spring. It was simply there, steady and reliable. The truth was that my family and all of our animals owed our daily hydration and cleansing to the small spring on the hill. There was a real sense of relationship to that spring because our needs were so real.

By contrast, most North Americans, who live in cities, are more distant from and less related to a particular source of water. Many urban North Americans may not know the source of the water they use in day-to-day life. The multiple sources of water and the complex, hidden water systems are more or less taken for granted. However, if the water main bursts, we are quickly reminded of our profound dependence on water and a steady, reliable source.

Christians have a water source too: the spring of baptism. This spring wells up from the depths of God. We introduce the service of baptism with these words:

> Through the Sacrament of Baptism
>   we are initiated into Christ's holy church.
> We are incorporated into God's mighty acts of salvation
>   and given new birth through water and the Spirit.
> All this is God's gift, offered without price.[15]

Christian initiation is symbolized and signed with the water of baptism. Through confirmation and reaffirmation of our faith, we renew and acknowledge what God has done and is doing for us (*UMH*, p. 33, No. 2). In baptism, God claims persons of all ages to belong to the covenant of God's new creation and to participate in Christ's royal priesthood (see *UMH*, p. 37, No. 11). Baptism is a given for Christians; it is the foundation of our life together as members of the body of Christ.

Holy baptism is a way—a specific, sacramental way—that God uses to act in our lives and to constitute the church. In baptism, God connects us to the mystery of Christ's dying and rising (Romans 6:3-11). In baptism, God marks us as disciples (Matthew 28:19) and pours out upon us the Holy Spirit and the forgiveness of sins (Acts 2:38). In baptism God washes us clean and sets us apart for life in the covenant community (Jeremiah 31:31-34; Mark 1:5; 1 Corinthians 12:13). In baptism, God erases all human distinctions and prideful exclusiveness, joining us as members of the body of Christ (Galatians 3:25-29; Ephesians 4:4-6). In baptism, we die to life without God (Romans 6:3) and are born of water and the Spirit (John 3:3-8). Through baptism, we are born anew into a living hope and made part of a "chosen race, a royal priesthood, a holy nation, God's own people, in order that you may proclaim the mighty acts of him who called you out of darkness into his marvelous light" (see 1 Peter 2:9). Scripture affirms a vital connection between baptism and the transformation of people and the formation of the church.[16] The spring of God's mercy and grace wells up for a thirsty and needy people.

Yet we tend to see baptism as a thing of little consequence. We tend to see it as something we do, a ritual with little connection to anything real or vital, and as an embarrassing vestige of the past.[17] Church leaders have allowed baptism to be a mere footnote in our life together, and we have paid little attention to what God has done and is doing in and through this means of grace.

What if the church ceased arguing about the doctrine of baptism and began to trust God to do what Scripture and tradition say God longs to do among a baptized and baptizing people? We are living on the edge of an emerging mission frontier where all around us people are searching for God and for meaning, belonging, healing, and hope. Baptism, as a means of God's gracious action, is at the heart of our essential ministry to searching, longing people. This book proposes a way of embedding baptism into the essential ministry of your congregation.

## RECLAIMING BAPTISM AND OUR WAYS OF *KNOWING*

For some readers, the first response to this call to a revitalized appreciation of the significance of baptism may be less than enthusiastic. You may argue that baptism, for yourself and for others, is a singularly unmemorable event and of little meaning. You may wish it was otherwise, but this is the case. You may, on theological grounds, object that viewing baptism as a key moment in the life and ministry of the congregation is dangerously close to putting our trust in ritual acts. There is a great deal of unrest about and reexamination of the theology, meaning, and practice of the sacrament of baptism in the church today.[18]

Our theological and emotional discomfort with the significance of baptism would be surprising to Christians of the third and fourth centuries.[19] Read the baptismal sermons of Theodore of Mopsuestia or Cyril of Jerusalem, and you will find a dynamic sense of what God does in baptism. With other early Christians, they held that both the benefits of Christ's passion and resurrection and the promise of God's reign were applied as each person was baptized. Theodore said:

> These things only happen to us in symbols, but St. Paul wishes to make it clear [reference to Romans 6:5] that we are *not concerned with empty symbols but with realities,* in which we profess our faith with longing and without hesitation.[20]

Theodore understood that in baptism, God was at work to bring about the realities of transforming grace. In response to these realities, the newly baptized, with all the believers, passionately professed their faith.

Keep in mind that congregations in the third and fourth centuries surrounded baptism with a vital process of forming people in the basics of faith and discipleship. The congregation structured its life in ways that made disciples. (See the narrative in the introduction, pp. 10-12.) For the sake of God and those searching for God, how can your congregation recover this dynamic experience of baptism?

While it is beyond the scope and purpose of this volume to discuss every aspect of these matters, there is one issue that we must examine here. In a word, the issue is the way we know. The tradition of contemporary Western thought and education views people, things, places, and actions as facts and objects. This is in remarkable contrast to the way and wisdom of the spiritual tradition of the Bible and the early church. The truth is that we are more the children of modern philosophy (the Enlightenment) than we are children of the biblical and early-church tradition. The Enlightenment's legacy to the modern way of knowing lies in its creation of a distance between the knower and the known. This objectification of the world keeps reality out there so that it makes no demands upon the knower. The modern world knows out of curiosity and the desire to control and possess. Our intellectual tradition educates us to know with the eye of the mind. The world and others exist as objects of our seeing and control. We prize facts because the knower does not have to become involved.

By contrast, in the Bible and the early church, persons knew with the heart and with life, as well as with the mind—that is with a sense of relationship, participation, and consequence. In the biblical way of knowing, a person is transformed because he or she is known by the truth. For a familiar sample of this way of knowing, read Psalm 139. The Psalmist is amazed, overwhelmed, filled with praise, and secure in the experience of being known by God. The psalm ends not with speculation about God, but with an invitation for God to search and to lead the psalmist's heart and thoughts:

> Search me, O God, and know my heart,
>     test me and know my thoughts.
> See if there is any wicked way in me,
>     and lead me in the way everlasting.
> *Psalm 139:23-24*

In this way of knowing, persons, places, and actions are not mere shells of reality; they are present with the presence of a *thou*, to use Martin Buber's term. In this way of knowing and being known, truth cannot be known without participation and transformation. This is why your congregation's rediscovery of baptism must come within the context of the total flow of God's grace. Baptism does not and cannot stand alone. Like a jewel, baptism needs a setting. Your congregation can set the sacrament of baptism in the ring of its reaching out, welcoming, forming, nurturing, and sending actions.

Parker Palmer, a contemporary educator and contemplative, contrasts the language of our modern intellectual tradition (reality, facts, theory, objectivity) with the language of spiritual knowledge (truth, relationship, community, transformation, troth, commitment).[21] Using Palmer's model, baptism as fact is quite different from baptism as truth.

In the fact way of knowing, baptism is a moment in time, a ritual text said, and a ritual act done. It is a fact with no real connection to other objects in the world. In the baptism-as-truth approach, baptism is a covenant—a relationship with us entered into by God in Christ within God's community and sealed with the Holy Spirit (Titus 3:4-7).

As a living truth baptism is an action in which we are transformed by knowing that we were known and that we were called before we knew. This is the powerful insight of infant baptism. Before the baby can do anything, God claims the child for a relationship. Our baptism is a truth. God has chosen and claimed us for a continuing relationship and transformation. Viewed as truth, baptism touches the totality of our being and places us within a gracious community of caring people and a network of accountability for a way of life. Baptism as truth is not so much an event as a process that began before we entered the waters and will continue throughout our lives. In baptism, God calls us to a quest for the truth that has tracked us as Francis Thompson's hound of heaven and as the widow searching for her lost coin in Luke 15.

The current anxiety of the church in the modern world feels like a storm, but our anchor is God. With a grace that tethers us to the possibility of coming home (prevenient grace), God allows us to feel the pain of our disconnectedness and discontent. Allowing us to feel our anxiety, God is prompting the church into a fresh search for the river that makes glad the city of God. The tether of grace will not let us go. Neither will the Spirit give up on the ways God has given to empower us to see with both mind and heart the connection of all things in heaven and on earth (Ephesians 1:9-10). We may have lost a sense of the vitality of baptism, but God has not.

## NOT A PEBBLE IN A BOX, BUT A BRANCH ON A TREE

Baptism need not be a cold, perfunctory ritual, nor an empty symbol. Rather, in the ancient way of knowing, it is a deeply personal, communal, and organic truth. Martin Thornton writes, "We are in Christ, not as a pebble in a box but as a branch on a tree."[22] When the church invites us to remember the truth of our baptism, the invitation is to remember that we have been grafted into Christ as one of his own. The invitation is to remember the deep connection that empowers us to say to the other branches, "With you, the whole church, I am liberated from chaos. With you, I have been visited by the Spirit, who broods over the floods of my life. With you, I have made my passage through the Red Sea of sin and death. With you, I have been to the Jordan and crossed into the land of promise. With you and for the sake of the world, I have been crucified with Christ. Yet with you, I live! I share the covenant given in the life-giving water of Christ. With you, I share in the mystery of God and the ministry of Jesus. Thanks be to God!"

What if your congregation's life and outreach served as a setting for people to experience such connection, faith, passion, joy, and confidence? Our participation in the baptismal covenant can be an animating gift when remembered and reaffirmed in the larger context of all that God is doing in the world and in the church. Gayle Felton puts it this way:

> Baptism, then, is not so much an event as it is process. Like the Christian life for which it is both empowerment and metaphor, baptism is dynamic, not static; a journey, not a destination; a quest, not an acquisition. Baptism is promise, the fulfilling of which requires a lifetime and beyond. It is prolepsis—representing in the now that which will be accomplished in the future, but representing that anticipated fruition so powerfully as to make it real even now.[23]

When Martin Luther touched his forehead and affirmed, "I am baptized," he was affirming his faith in the faithfulness of God in Christ. In his affirmation of his relationship to God, Luther was not like Ponce de Leon looking for a mythical spring; he was trusting in the promise of God, given reliably in the baptismal covenant. Whether facing fierce opponents in the church or dark voices within, Luther repeatedly affirmed the living and life-giving relationship given in baptism. He knew the assurance of being known by the God who forgave him and cared for him unto everlasting life.

While this look at baptism may not have resolved your concerns and questions, I hope that it has helped you to consider that baptism is much more than mere fact or matter-of-fact ritual. I hope that this exploration makes clear that baptism must be seen in a larger context and not in isolation. Baptism is not just about distinctly different things: water, words, ideas, church buildings, rivers or fonts, people to be enrolled as members, certificates, clergy, and congregation. Rather, baptism is about the deep connection God works in the truth and power of Jesus Christ for our conversion and entrance into the faith community that shares in God's new creation.

The recent revisions of the services of the baptismal covenant seek to recover the sense of baptism as transforming truth and as covenant made and reaffirmed again and again in worship and witness. The question before us now is this: How can the truth and power of what God does in baptism be embedded in the congregation's essential ministry in the emerging missionary context? In the remainder of this book, we will explore a vision of what baptism set in the congregation's essential ministry might look like. We will outline a process for this approach to congregational life and witness on the new missionary frontier.

---

## BASIC CONCEPTS IN CHAPTER TWO

❧ In a time of rapid and profound change, the church is searching for fresh sources for vital ministry.

❧ Baptism as God's act and the baptismal covenant as the source and setting for our initial and continuing response are basic to faithful discipleship and vitality in the faith community.

❧ This resource invites a new look at baptism in connection with the congregation's essential ministry.

❧ Modern approaches to truth are so cognitive and rationalistic that they have dulled our sensitivity to the ways God meets us, knows us, and claims us for relationship.

❧ Biblical and early church approaches to truth are holistic, personal, transforming, and covenantal.

Chapter Three

# CHRISTIAN INITIATION AND THE CONGREGATION

C hristian initiation is rooted in the worship life of the community of faith. It is not a catechism class with a pastor, nor is it a short course in Christianity led by a teacher or a team of teachers. Rather than a catalog of content items to be learned and digested by candidates, this approach uses a series of stages and ritual actions through which the congregation and candidates move toward baptism.

The approach embraces a process of incorporation rather than a single point of ritual celebration. It requires the action of all the parts of the body working together (1 Corinthians 12). *The United Methodist Book of Worship* speaks of the congregation's corporately sponsoring each candidate and taking seriously the vows made at each baptism. "When someone is baptized, it is a crucial event in the life both of that person and of the Church. What happens to that member of the body of Christ will make a difference to every other member, and the rest of the Church can never again be the same" (UMBOW, 83).

This statement becomes even more powerful if read in light of family systems theory. When a baby is born into a family, seismic shifts take place. Older siblings feel displaced. Routines are upset, and new rituals are introduced. The resistance and struggle that take place in families is a good image for what happens in a congregation. This also explains why many churches that say they want to welcome new people do not grow: Growth and exercise of the congregation's essential ministry is subversive of the status quo.

Viewing your congregation's essential ministry with an understanding of the congregation as a system challenges the current practices of incorporating persons into the life of the faith community. How do congregations as a whole sponsor persons into the community of faith and take their communal vows seriously? Can such action be accomplished in the "twinkling of an eye" on a Sunday morning as a family gathers around the baptismal font? How does God use ritual to shape and incorporate people into the community of faith?

## CHRISTIAN INITIATION AS A PROCESS

Much of the present day confusion and struggle about baptism is due to the fact that we often see only the tip of the iceberg. When we speak of baptism, we immediately think of the event, the moment in time, the point at which water is applied and words are spoken. That visible point in experience often bears the full load of our awareness and reference to God's action and our response.

This point in time is only the tip of the larger reality of the baptismal covenant. Covenant is a crucial, operative word. This larger reality underlies and supports the baptismal event. This gracious reality includes, but is never exhausted by

- the scriptural texts and images of baptism;

- the history and experience of baptism in the church;

- the prevenient and justifying grace of God working in daily life and in the congregation to nurture each person toward baptism;

- the sanctifying action of the Spirit, which is still future to the event;

- the continuity of Christ's holy church, both universal and local, as the covenant community of the baptized.

The reality of this gracious, unfolding process is the ground of a broader understanding of baptism and initiation. This reality is more organic than organizational. The risen Lord gives the congregation the opportunity to embody this larger reality of the baptismal covenant in an ongoing way. In this way, the congregation participates in the work of God in Christ to birth new daughters and sons. The assembly enacts the hospitality of God's own grace with these words following baptism:

Pastor: Now it is our joy to welcome our new *sisters and brothers* in Christ.
People: **Through baptism**
**you are incorporated by the Holy Spirit**
**into God's new creation**
**and made to share in Christ's royal priesthood.**
**We are all one in Christ Jesus.**
**With joy and thanksgiving we welcome you**
**as *members* of the family of Christ.**[24]

The congregation's enactment of the baptismal covenant appropriately comes both before and after the event of baptism. Come to the Waters seeks to prompt your congregation's vision of how it will welcome and form persons before and after the rite of baptism itself. The stages and services of Christian initiation are designed to anticipate, nurture, and discern repentance and growing faithfulness in those embraced by the congregation's ministry. In and by the services of Christian initiation, the congregation seeks to communicate to the candidates that baptism is birth into a lifetime of repentance and conversion within a covenant community.

## THE INTEGRITY OF INITIATION, WELCOME, AND HOSPITALITY

The Services of the Baptismal Covenant (*UMH*, p. 32-54 and *UMBOW*, p. 81-114) contain a vision of the church and conversion that go far beyond the liturgy. Initiation is more than a ritual event. Christian initiation is the congregation's reaching out and receiving people, inviting, nurturing, and welcoming them into a pattern of appropriate spiritual formation. Initiation also entails opportunities to engage in ministry, learning, and fellowship that includes each person in the life and prayer of the church family. It is a continual encounter of the whole congregation with the Lord, who leads each of us into the community of faith.

The work of Christian initiation requires planning and coordination so that the congregation is able to continue its welcome and hospitality throughout the period of inquiry, hearing, candidacy, initiation, and post-baptismal reflection. (See "Ministries of Christian Initiation" in Chapter Four, p. 53.)

Unless Christian initiation is the work and expression of the whole congregation, it lacks integrity and short circuits the converting work of the Spirit. The essential ministry of your church is the task of the congregation as a whole. The community of faith must embrace and share in the ministry of all Christians to those who are being converted and initiated.

While it is true that some persons in the congregation will have more visible and intense responsibility for this process, all will love and pray for those who are invited to come to the waters. This ministry cannot be delegated to a few members, nor is it the sole responsibility and prerogative of ordained or other professional staff. Integrity requires that baptism be preceded by caring and welcome, instruction and nurture, guidance and reflection with the community of faith.

As when a new member of the family is added through birth or adoption, so new members in the church require the household of faith to prepare for, welcome and receive, and continually nurture them in the conversion and initiation process. As a new member of the family changes the family constellation, its routines, relationships, and activities, new persons in the church invite the congregational family to reshape its life to more faithfully receive, nurture, and form new members in the way of discipleship. The congregation must face and counter its resistance to new family members. In the same way that older siblings in a family need to be engaged in welcoming a new baby in order to overcome their feelings of displacement and to love their new brother or sister, so leaders can prompt the congregation to know and support those being born into the household of faith.

## A BASIC PATTERN FOR CHRISTIAN INITIATION

At this point, an outline of the process may help you to understand and visualize this approach to Christian initiation. The pattern consists of *four stages* of formation and instruction and *four services* of celebration that mark the transitions at the end of each stage. The process serves as an intentional bridge from evangelization, the start of conversion, to the ritual event of initiation, *baptism*, and on to full and ongoing participation in the life and ministry of God's people. While this outline of the basic pattern is modeled on the *catechesis* of the ancient and contemporary church, it seeks to describe the process with maximum flexibility so that congregations may adapt it to their settings.

The outline is brief. The details, particularly those of the worship services (1.1, 2.1, 3.1, 4.1) are elaborated in the resources in Part Two of this book.

## A BASIC PATTERN OF CHRISTIAN INITIATION

*Sponsors accompany candidates for baptism throughout the
journey; and the catechist (formation director)
working with the pastor, guides the process.*

### 1.0 INQUIRY STAGE

The work of evangelization leads into a period of inquiry that includes intentional, mutual storytelling and questioning about the life of faith. Trust is established, and the good news of invitation to life and relationship with Jesus Christ is presented through reflection upon the Scriptures. Inquirers, sponsors, the catechist, and the pastor engage in discernment of the inquirer's readiness for more thorough conversion and discipleship.

### 1.1 WELCOME SERVICE

This service celebrates the decision to follow Christ. The inquirers are introduced and welcomed by the congregation as hearers. The congregation invites each person to hear the word of God with them in weekly worship. (This service may occur at any time the inquirer is ready for the journey of conversion.)

*Actions and symbols in the service may include greeting inquirers at the door and
welcoming them, reading the Word of God, marking with the sign of the cross.*

### 2.0 FORMATION STAGE

This is an extended period of exploration, formation, and reflection with sponsors, the catechist, and the pastor. The stage is marked by engagement with the four basic components of formation: worship, reflection on Scripture, prayer, and ministry in daily life (including service to the poor and suffering). Experience followed by reflection is the approach of this stage and those that follow. The process is characterized by the hearer's growing ability to discern God's activity and call in the events of daily life.

### 2.1 CALLING TO BAPTISM

When there is discernment of readiness for baptism, the congregation celebrates growth by calling him or her as a candidate for baptism.[25] Usually this takes place on the first Sunday in Lent or the first Sunday in Advent.

*Actions and symbols in the service include a call of names,
an announcement of the date of baptism, and prayer.*

### 3.0 INTENSIVE PREPARATION STAGE

This intensive period includes examination of life, reflection on Scripture texts leading to baptism, congregational prayer for the candidates, and candidates' journeying with the congregation toward baptism and incorporation into the death and resurrection of Christ.

*Actions and symbols of this stage include presenting the faith and prayer of the church—The Apostle's Creed and The Lord's Prayer—and crying out for the candidates to be freed from their thirsts, blindness, and death.*

### 3.1 INITIATION

Preceded by intensive prayer, fasting, worship, and reflection, the candidates are initiated with baptism, laying on of hands, and Holy Communion.[26] Usually initiation takes place at Easter or on the Sunday commemorating the baptism of the Lord.

*Actions and symbols include baptism, laying on of hands, anointing, and the Eucharist.*

### 4.0 INTEGRATION STAGE

This period gives the newly baptized time to enter more fully into the life of the community of faith. The stage is marked by deep reflection on the experience of initiation and on participation in the life and mission of the church. As before, the readings of Scripture in worship are central to reflection on the sacraments and on the vocation of discipleship. The stage may also include discernment of spiritual gifts and continuing clarification of ministry in daily life.

### 4.1 AFFIRMATION OF MINISTRY IN THE WORLD

The congregation recognizes and celebrates the witness and ministry of the newly baptized. The congregation prays for them and affirms their participation in ministries of the Body of Christ.

There are strong reasons for structuring this process around the Lent-Easter-Pentecost cycle of the Christian year. This will be discussed in Chapters Six and Seven.

Further on in this chapter, we will consider the need for adaptation of this basic pattern. (See p. 37.)

## RITUAL ACTION AND SEEING

You have undoubtedly noticed that worship is an important component of the basic pattern of Christian initiation. For many North Americans, the word *ritual* conjures up images of empty ceremonies that few understand or appreciate. This sense of dead ritual arises no doubt when ritual practices get separated from the personal and interpersonal reality of our relationships with God and with one another. One of the objectives of this book is to recover and celebrate the role of ritual that is empowered by the Holy Spirit to open, shape, reveal, and transform our life together in the body of Christ.

The word *ritual* is derived from the word *rite,* meaning a formal procedure, custom, or habit. A ritual act is a simple action that may or may not involve words. The Holy Spirit can and does use ritual actions to open up the eyes of the mind and heart. The usefulness of ritual in the hands of the Spirit lies in the juxtaposition of words, space, people, story, sound, movement, music, and ordinary things like water, bread, and cup. A ritual act is also an action that can be repeated and is usually recognizable because it has been repeated.[27] The repetition of the act is an avenue that the Spirit can use to connect past experiences of faith with Scripture and with the ever new circumstances of living and growing faith.

For example, children love the ritual of bedtime. As most parents know, their children have a playful, but solemn, sense of order about their bedtime ritual. Do you remember a story, a good-night prayer up close, blankets tucked in around the neck, a kiss on the forehead, and those special words? Then it's lights out. The ritual of bedtime orders the end of the day, deepens the parent-child relationship, and serves as prelude to sleep.

Ordinary daily life in all human communities (family, church, government, social organizations, businesses) is punctuated by rituals that order and facilitate the connections and relationships for a given time and space. By opening the venetian blinds in the morning we make a ritual of our acceptance of a new day. Grace said before meals deepens our sense of need and the mystery of provision from God's hand in creation and through the work of others.

We have seasonal rituals. How do you know when it is Thanksgiving day? The calendar says so! Yes, but there is a much deeper, primal level of knowing it is Thanksgiving day. The heart and body know it is Thanksgiving when the smell of turkey begins to waft through the house, when the silver and special dishes are on the family table, when Uncle Bill and Aunt Carrie knock on the front door. Ritual brings together bodies, senses, and relationships in the context of time.

For the church, the time we celebrate is God's time. We keep time with Christ using ordinary things in light of the sacred story. By ritual action, we claim the promises of God for ourselves and for all the world. Even the gathering of the congregation at 10:30 A.M. every Sunday morning is a ritual act. That act, even if no further actions or words are used, is a powerful sign of a participation in something that orders all of the week that follows.

## SEEKERS AND THE WORSHIPING CONGREGATION

What congregations have to offer inquirers and seekers is the reality of ongoing worship and life as disciples of Jesus. Weekly, in Scripture reading, sermon, prayer, and Holy Communion, Christians encounter the risen Lord. The actions of gathering, praising, forgiving and being forgiven, remembering, proclaiming, sharing a holy meal, and going out are at the heart of who we are as God's people. All of these actions are animated by God's Spirit and are responses to Christ, who is present among us. Our gathering is a public act and a public art, not a secret meeting of insiders.

Thus, far from being disconnected with life, the full range of our human experience during the week is offered, shaped, and organized in and by the rituals of Christian worship. In ritual action, our day-to-day experience is continually interpreted by the Spirit of God. In the drama of corporate worship, we know anew "whether we live or whether we die, we are the Lord's" (Romans 14:8). In worship, God reorders and reconnects us to one another and to Jesus, the risen Lord; so that all of life, even our doubt and quest for truth, belongs to God. Into this public, weekly gathering, congregations welcome persons to a journey from an old reality to a new reality in the context of their faith experience of Christ.

Just as the rituals of grief (including the visitation, memorial or funeral service, burial, and post-funeral meals) allow the larger community to journey with the bereaved, so the weekly worship of Christians allows them to accompany seekers on their journey. Just as rituals of engagement, showers, premarital counseling, wedding arrangements, rehearsals, weddings, and wedding parties give the community a way of supporting and participating in the journey of the couple, so the rites of Christian initiation create settings for the congregation to walk with people toward baptism.

For persons who have not been baptized and who have little or no formation within the community of faith, the event of baptism is remote. They are strangers in a foreign land. Offering them an hour of consultation or a four week membership class is inadequate, if not cruel. It leaves them unprepared, uninformed, and unformed in the symbols and relationships of a new realm. They are persons without a language, without images and stories with which to understand and communicate. They have no way to make sense of their experience.

By contrast, the weekly hearing of Scripture in a communal, ritual context not only prepares persons to be initiated, the Holy Spirit uses it to organize and order their experience in daily life. Shared worship allows faith to be formed and commitments to be made that are consistent with God's converting action. Inquirers and hearers are formed as they learn, alongside believers, the disciplines of living the Christian life. Worship that is solidly rooted in the Christian tradition, open to our human journeys, and empowered by the Holy Spirit can serve to initiate and transform people in ever deeper and richer ways. The early church spoke of this journey as a leaving Egypt.

"A Basic Pattern of Christian Initiation" and the resources in Part Two are designed to help your congregation welcome people who are seeking God, and offer them a path by which to find their place in the church's story and ministry. On this path, your congregation will enable others to discover that their time is reshaped into the church's time and that their story converges with Christ's story.

## ADAPTING THIS BASIC PATTERN

You, the reader, will no doubt quickly recognize that one size does not fit all. Clearly, there are many persons for whom this pattern is not appropriate. The church affirms the inclusiveness of the baptismal covenant for persons of any age and offers specific guidance for the practice of baptismal inclusiveness.[28] (See UMBOW, pp. 81-84.)

Congregations are not called to create barriers for those God is drawing to faith and to the reign of God. Flexibility and adaptation of the pattern of adult candidacy for baptism is essential.

One size does not fit all. Consider the following persons. What do they need?

❧ infants born into churched families;

❧ infants born into non-churched families;

❧ children of parents who are themselves in the process of conversion;

❧ youth and adults baptized as infants or children, but without the experience of conversion beyond that point;

❧ persons baptized in infancy or early childhood who have not made a first reaffirmation of the baptismal covenant (confirmation);

❧ faithful members of other denominations who are seeking membership in The United Methodist Church;

❧ adults or youth whose Christian experience following baptism causes them to desire a sacramental event that recognizes a significant experience or decision;

❧ lapsed members;

❧ members of the congregation who want to reaffirm the baptismal covenant on special days of the Christian year, especially Easter Vigil or Easter Day, Pentecost, All Saints, and the Baptism of the Lord.

The services and prayers that appear in Part Two of this book provide options based on the basic pattern described in this chapter. "Services for the Initiation of Adults" reflect the description given in the basic pattern above and is the pattern from which the options are developed. "Services for the Initiation of Children" and "Services for Members Returning to the Baptismal Covenant" are designed to accommodate persons whose age or experience requires a variation of the basic pattern. Pastors and other leaders are encouraged to adapt the model services and prayers to support the formation and conversion of all who are seeking God and life in the community of faith.

The chart on page 43 shows the progression of the basic pattern and two primary adaptations. Appropriate times during the Christian year are indicated.

## CHALLENGING ASSUMPTIONS

The approach to Christian initiation proposed in this book is more than a slight mid-course adjustment for most congregations. This proposal is a radical change. It challenges beliefs and assumptions held by many congregations and leaders, some of which are:

- ❧ Evangelism, formation, and guidance are tasks that are largely separate from the worship life of the church.

- ❧ Baptism is a mere formality to be done in the course of receiving members.

- ❧ Receiving members should happen in as short a time as possible.

- ❧ Preparation for baptism or confirmation should be of minimal inconvenience to the candidates.

- ❧ Pastors carry the responsibility for forming and nurturing disciples.

- ❧ Any time of the year when persons are ready for baptism or confirmation or reception into the church is as appropriate as any other.

- ❧ Readiness for baptism, confirmation, or membership is determined by completion of a class or course of instruction and/or by the pastor's judgment.

- ❧ Sponsors and godparents are cosmetic trappings in the process of preparing persons for baptism or for reaffirmation of baptismal vows

- ❧ Sponsors and godparents need only to stand with the candidates during the celebration of baptism, confirmation, reception.

- ❧ Evangelism, formation, and initiation are specialized functions in the local congregation rather than a way of living as a congregation.

- ❧ Adding new members is something that happens automatically without a plan and a process for conversion.

These are some of the assumptions that are called into question by this approach. Now we can turn to consideration of basic understandings that underlie the process of Christian initiation.

## PRINCIPLES THAT UNDERLIE CHRISTIAN INITIATION

When a congregation and its leaders adopt this approach they should do so with a clear understanding of the supporting principles upon which it is based. While these have been implied above, it may be helpful to make them explicit here.

1. Christian initiation is grounded in the services of the baptismal covenant (*UMH*, pp. 33-54 and *UMBOW*, pp. 81-114) as the sacrament of dying and rising with Jesus Christ. The foundation and power of the baptismal covenant is the faithfulness of God in Christ. Christian initiation points to and relies upon the converting grace of God at work through the church and in the world.

2. Christian initiation is an invitation for people to approach baptism or reaffirmation using several steps raised by the service of baptism itself. "Do you renounce the spiritual forces of wickedness? Do you repent of your sin? Do you confess Jesus Christ as your Savior? Do you put your whole trust in his grace? Do you promise to serve him as your Lord?" Candidates need time and guidance in preparing to answer these questions.

3. Christian initiation assumes and requires that the whole congregation will engage in the work of reaching out, welcoming, forming faith and discipleship, and sending persons out to ministry in daily life.

4. Christian initiation is compatible in structure with the calendar of the Christian Year, particularly the Lent, Easter, and the Great Fifty Days cycle. Congregations may adapt this schema to other times of the year, such as the Advent, Christmas, Epiphany, and Baptism of the Lord cycle.

5. Christian initiation engages many persons in special roles that represent and make personal the congregation's caring, prayers, formation, and guidance.

6. Christian initiation requires careful, long-range planning and leadership.

7. Christian initiation requires sponsors for each inquirer. Sponsors serve as mentors throughout journey of conversion.

8. Christian initiation assumes that readiness for baptism or reaffirmation of baptismal vows will be based on mutual discernment. The candidate, the sponsor, and the catechist collaborate toward discernment, under the guidance of the pastor(s).

## ARTIFACT OF THE FUTURE:
## THE *CATECHUMENATE* AS A WORK OF GRACE

Words with more than three syllables intimidate most people. The four syllable word *catechumen* (cat-e-kiu-men) is especially intimidating because it has no syllable resembling any ordinary word we use in daily speech. Yet it is a word that makes an important technical connection for people who are intent on the essential ministry of making disciples.

The Greek root of *catechumen* is related to our word *echo*, which suggests the early Christian sense of the term. The catechumens were persons being instructed in the Word of God in such a way that the risen Lord echoed in both their thought and conduct. In Acts 18:24, Apollos is described as "an eloquent man, well-versed in the scriptures." The following verse accounts for his formation in the Scriptures: "He had been instructed in the Way of the Lord; and he spoke with burning enthusiasm and taught accurately the things concerning Jesus" (Acts 18:25). The Greek word for instructed is *catekiumenos* (cat-e-kiu-men-os).

The text emphasizes the intensity and depth of instruction and formation Apollos had experienced. Note also that his instruction was in the Way of the Lord as a manner of life and not as a mere acceptance of concepts and abstract ideas. The instruction had resulted in transformation and a deep commitment. It is also worthy of note that Apollos is seen as needing to continue in formation for "he knew only the baptism of John" (Acts 18:25). While the story does not tell us when or how Apollos learned of baptism into Jesus, the evidence in 1 Corinthians 1 suggests that he was further instructed and baptized.

The catechumenate *(cat-e-kiu-men-ate)*, as a structure for formation and instruction in preparation for baptism, may appear to be a fossil, an inflexible anachronism of history. The language of Christian initiation may provoke thoughts of rigid forms and cookie-cutter processes. Precisely the opposite is the case. The "catechumenate" may be thought of as an artifact from the future.[29] If the risen Lord is always coming to us from the future, then the work of grace in each person's life is a unique participation in the coming reign of God. Formation and instruction allow the Word to reverberate in the ears, heart, and life of each candidate in a unique and personal way.

The journey toward faith begins as personal experience. The Holy Spirit brings the good news to persons where they are and as they are. When they begin to relate to a congregation, they need to be welcomed with hospitality and graciously led in conversation and prayer. A flexible attentiveness expresses hospitality to the stranger.

If the process has a clear vision and is understood, its forms and steps will be flexible and adaptable for the sake of Christ's work in each person. Christian initiation is not about giving answers to questions inquirers are not asking. It is not about packaging their experience within tidy rituals. Christian initiation is about meeting people where they are, listening to them in their hurts and hopes, and sharing with them the great hope that is in the community of faith. (See pp. 48-50)

A recent study of growing Lutheran congregations suggests that obligation, or a sense of responsibility to traditional forms, is not one of the main reasons that people in our changing culture participate in church life. "When people seek [and participate in] a congregation, it is the one that ministers to their needs [that they will choose]. Most often they come with needs that are not [obviously] matters of faith."[30] This does not mean that forms, processes, and rituals are unimportant or that they are to be casually discarded. It does mean that we follow Jesus by keeping the focus on people. It also means that the vital congregation welcomes seekers just as they are and in ways that help them to see how their needs connect with matters of faith. Participation in worship, reflection on the biblical texts in small groups with sponsors, telling faith stories, and focusing on ministry in daily life make those connections evident.

Pastors, sponsors, and other leaders are agents of the Spirit as they hear the concerns, questions, and stories of people seeking God. The processes of Christian initiation can help your congregation welcome the Jeremys and Lauras we met in the last chapter. Using this approach, the congregation invites seekers to tell their stories, to be heard, and to discover in the church's hospitality the compassion and presence of God. In and by discipleship, the congregation seeks to communicate to inquirers and hearers that the sacrament of baptism is birth into a lifetime of enacting the journey of Christian initiation, and that conversion is entrance into a community of people who live by water and the Spirit.

## BASIC CONCEPTS IN CHAPTER THREE

1. Baptism is an event in time and part of the larger reality of growing in grace that precedes and follows it.

2. The Services of the Baptismal Covenant call the congregation to welcome, care for, love, and pray for persons both before and after the event of baptism.

3. A basic pattern of Christian initiation consists of a series of four stages of formation and preparation and four services of celebration that mark the end of each stage and entry into the next.

4. The Spirit of God attracts and shapes seekers through the ritual gathering and the public action of the church in its worship of the triune God.

5. The basic pattern is adaptable for persons who do not fit the norm of adults preparing for baptism. There are two primary forms of adaptation: preparation of families presenting infants and children for baptism, and preparation of returning members for reaffirmation of the baptismal covenant.

6. The process of Christian initiation is flexible in relationship to the needs and questions of persons on the journey of conversion. Guidance and instruction are essential and shaped according to the needs of persons being formed for a life of discipleship.

## Adaptation of the Initiation Process—An Outline

*italics indicate a ritual action or service.*

| Initiation of Adults | Initiation of Infants and Young Children with Preparation of Their Families | Baptized Persons Returning to the Baptismal Covenant |
|---|---|---|
| 1. Outreach and Inquiry | 1. Parent's Inquiry Concerning Baptism | 1. Outreach and Inquiry |
| 2. *Welcome of Hearers* | 2. *Welcome of Children as Hearers Through the Parents* | 2. *Welcome of Returning Members* |
| 3. Formation | 3. With Parents, Formation for Baptism | 3. Formation in Faith and Ministry |
| 4. *Calling Persons to Baptism* **(1st Sunday in Lent or 1st Sunday in Advent)** | 4. *Calling Children to Baptism Through the Parents* **(1st Sunday in Lent or 1st Sunday in Advent)** | 4. *Calling the Baptized to Continuing Conversion* **(Ash Wednesday)** |
| 5. Intensive Preparation for Baptism **(during Lent or Advent)** | 5. Intensive Preparation for Baptism With the Family **(during Lent or Advent)** | 5. Intensive Preparation for Affirmation of the Baptismal Covenant **(during Lent)** |
| 6. *Full Initiation/Holy Baptism* **(Easter Vigil or Baptism of the Lord)** | 6. *Full Initiation/Holy Baptism* **(Easter Vigil or Baptism of the Lord)** | 6. *Celebration of Reconciliation* **(Holy Thursday)** *and Reaffirmation* **(Easter)** |
| 7. Post-Baptismal Formation and Integration into the Life and Mission of the Church **(during the Great Fifty Days or during the Sundays after Epiphany)** | 7. Post-Baptismal Formation and Integration into the Life and Mission of the Church **(For children this is more gradual and much longer, extends until they are able to profess their faith in adolescence or adulthood)** | 7. Integration into the Life and Mission of the Church **(during the Great Fifty Days)** |
| 8. *Affirmation of Ministry* **(Pentecost Sunday or Transfiguration Sunday)** | 8. *Confirmation and Affirmation of Ministry* **(Pentecost Sunday or Transfiguration Sunday)** | 8. *Affirmation of Ministry* **(Pentecost Sunday)** |

Chapter Four

# MINISTRY AND MINISTRIES THAT WELCOME SEEKERS

*"Without us, God will not. Without God, we cannot."*
Augustine of Hippo

Christian initiation is an approach suited for the emerging mission frontier. It originated in the first four centuries of the church as a missionary structure grounded in the worship and daily life of the Christian community. The present day North American church is recovering the process for its welcome of people seeking God in the emerging missionary context.[31]

There is a fresh urgency to make the good news of Jesus Christ accessible to seekers. Many adults today are thoroughly oriented to a pluralistic, post-modern relativism in their experience and outlook. The emergence of secularism in the 1960's and the more recent emergence of a religious pluralism in North America has resulted in increasing numbers of persons who have a spiritual base that is completely distinct from the Christian tradition. Styles of ministry and church life that served the fading missional context need to be evaluated and retooled for the current and emerging realities of our post-modern cultural context. How can your congregation reshape itself to serve seekers in this cultural setting?

## CHANGE AND ANXIETY

As we enter a new millennium, many pastors and church leaders experience an unsettling anxiety about the task and role of the church. When we consider the pace of change in the culture around us and the building pressure on the congregation to effectively respond, we feel like a big earthquake is coming. No wonder there is anxiety! The pressure upon leaders to cast a vision and to offer effective direction in our changing cultural context continues to build. The anxiety that comes with change is amplified because today's pastors and congregations have three basic options from which to choose:

1. The first option (Post-World War II Religion) is attractive because it is what has worked for us and it is familiar. The slogan of the 1950's and 60's was *Attend the church of your choice.* Post World War II religion in North America was institutional, optimistic, and voluntary. People joined churches as part of their

civic and community life. The values of the church were closely tied to the values of the nation. Church life was focused on programs and activities. Pastors were trained to serve the church in a stable and compatible cultural context. This option relied heavily on professionals to do the work of the church for the members. Ministry was largely seen as what happens in the church and in church activities. It was assumed that most people were Christian or sympathetic to Christian teaching. There was a truce between church and state; a soft compact of non-interference and protection. Continuing the success of the past is the agenda for those who cling to this option.

2. The second option (Post-Modern Apostolic Christianity) is a disciple-making and disciple-deploying model. It is and will be unattractive because it is unfamiliar to much of the current church that is largely oriented to the Post-World War II Religion approach. Post-Modern Apostolic Christianity is just beginning to emerge and is largely untested and untried. In this approach, church life focuses on the means of grace, making disciples, the ministry of the baptized, membership for mission, and solidarity with the poor and marginalized. The cry of this movement is "Unleash the church!" Post-modern Apostolic congregations require pastors who see themselves as leaders of mission outposts in a culture that is clearly not grounded in Christian discipleship. Conversion means formation and in-depth encounter with Christ in a religious tradition which is an alternative to the dominant culture. Continuous learning, innovation rooted in the gospel, and realistic understanding of the culture shapes leaders of these missionary congregations. Leaders focus on the essential ministry of the congregation and are clear about ministry as the work of the people in the world. Ministry focuses on people and not on programs and institutional agendas.

3. The third possibility (the Culturally Accessible Church) appears to have an immediate attractiveness in its imitation of the successful innovation of other churches. There are a growing number of large, fast growing, and innovative congregations in North America. These cutting edge churches tend to embrace the surrounding culture's media and methods in order to be accessible to seekers and those disenchanted with traditional churches. The innovations are seen as the reason for the success of these congregations, and many church leaders are attempting to learn from and imitate these approaches. Note: this movement is having considerable success by certain standards and cannot be dismissed as merely pandering to the culture or a focusing on numbers. The critical issue will be whether congregations that adopt this approach will succeed in making and deploying disciples for the love of God and of neighbor. Many of these congregations serve as centers for training (Willow Creek; Saddleback Community Church; The Crystal Cathedral; The Church of Joy; Ginghamsburg United Methodist in Tipp City, Ohio; and others) and offer schools for those who want to learn their ways. These churches have strong appeal because they are zealously focused on reaching out to people and have grown rapidly.[32]

In the near future, many congregations and leaders will stay with the first option. Continuing to operate as outposts of the enlightenment will be the course of least resistance in many situations. Leaders whose training, experience, and setting appear to be compatible with this passing era in North American culture will continue to use the Post-World War II Religion model. They will maintain peaceful coexistence with the cultural context and rely heavily upon professionals to do the work of the church.

In contrast to this, many congregations will explore the third option. The Culturally Accessible Church model is relatively young and continuously evolving. One thing is sure: For mainline denominations, there will be much controversy around this approach; and we will learn a great deal from congregations that embrace the culture's media and language. A major concern related to this option is whether or not these cutting-edge approaches tend to fix seekers at an entry level and harness them to a narrow political agenda as a substitute for service to God and neighbor. Time will tell. For the near future, this option will have a high profile in the range of possible approaches to ministry in a new millennium.

Without apology, this resource affirms the second option, the disciple-making, disciple-deploying model. This option recognizes the changes going on in the culture and is intent on welcoming people who are seeking God, forming them as disciples, and supporting and sending them out for lives of service and witness in the world. The disciple-making model has its risks also. Its way of weaving proclamation, worship, and ministry together in daily life as intentional obedience to Jesus can be greeted with any one of three negative responses: Some will see it as too difficult. Others may see it as irrelevant. Still others will consider it subversive. Such resistance is to be expected and there is some truth in each response. At the same time, the disciple-making, disciple-deploying option has much to commend it in the emerging missionary context.

Congregations choosing from these three models will exist side by side for the foreseeable future. This book's vision is rooted in the disciple-making and ministry-of-the-baptized model. Leaders and congregations who seek to implement Christian initiation as an expression of this essential ministry should be clear about the choice and its risks.

## MEMBERSHIP ORIENTATION AND CHRISTIAN INITIATION

Christian communities need radically different approaches for proclaiming the gospel in our post-modern culture. In this regard, it is important to distinguish between membership orientation and Christian initiation.

In the mid-1950's, when congregations received persons who were part of a Christian culture, membership classes provided necessary orientation for people to fit into the local church—its organization, its fellowship, and its programs. In a sense, this was and is a necessary part of helping persons feel at home in the congregation. In our current cultural context, however, if this is the sum total of what we offer persons seeking the life of faith and prayer, we badly short-change the gospel and the persons we incorporate into the faith community.

Membership orientation fails to serve the gospel and seekers if it lacks a vital foundation in the holy catholic church and adequate formation in the basics of Christian discipleship. It is a dry well, gathering persons around an organization or program or personality. Membership orientation lacks a connection to the transforming grace of Christ celebrated and welcomed in baptism. Membership orientation along these lines treats the church as an end in itself, whether or not this is intended. Viewed in light of the emerging mission frontier, if membership classes focus only on the institution and its traditions and programs, classes will be little more than advertising sessions for securing new recruits to secure the support of our congregations.

Christian initiation, on the other hand, is a process that gathers around the living Lord persons seeking faith and incorporates them into the coming reign of God. Its ecclesial base is the baptismal covenant by which persons are given a new identity in relationship to Christ, in his life, death, and resurrection. At the same time, Christian initiation is not merely a spiritual journey. The process takes place within a faith community and grounds the seeker in the worship and life of the congregation as a concrete expression of the whole church. The congregation initiates persons into the essential ministry of reaching out, welcoming, worshiping, nurturing, and sending. The end is not the congregation or the denomination; the end is the transforming gospel and God's new creation.

## NO MORE *PIRANHAS*

The Amazon, flowing to the Atlantic Ocean, may not suggest great danger to the casual observer. It looks peaceful and benign. The uninformed swimmer would discover otherwise upon entering the river.

Few congregations see themselves as carnivorous. They have no intention of being rapacious and predatory. Yet to culturally distant seekers, institutionally focused processes of gaining members can be more like piranhas than we realize.

If the membership class approach tends to perceive people as ready-made prospects for joining our congregations and denominations, Christian initiation processes call us to see and attend to people as persons to whom Jesus is listening with transforming grace. Christian initiation calls for a listening style of ministry: listening to seekers and listening for the voice of God that calls them and us into the transforming good news of Jesus Christ.

Listening does not mean that we only listen. We listen with the goal of making disciples and of persons discovering the transforming love of God. In a real sense, the emphasis on listening is a corrective for our dependence on talking as a way of telling the good news of Christ.

Our culture, with its orientation to marketing and sales, is anxious to convince and persuade others. In our task-oriented world, listening seems like a passive response to people. It seems to lack initiative. Just the thought of listening to others makes many of us nervous and tense. Who has time to listen? We have agendas and bottom lines to consider. We are used to meeting others with specific results in view.

Yet we all know the experience of "being had." Every adult knows the experience of being talked at, verbally pushed, manipulated, and pressured to buy something we did not want. Jesus calls us to a different way of being with people.

## JESUS AND LISTENING TO PEOPLE

The way of Jesus as listener is in marked contrast to the worst of our anxieties about growing churches and recruiting new members. Jesus listened to people as a contemplative listens. He saw people with both his mind and his heart. The striking thing that emerges in reflection on Jesus' way of knowing people is that he did not know them in order to sell them a product or to persuade them to join a cause.

In his encounter with the woman at the well (John 4), Jesus listened at a remarkable depth. In the interchange, she told him of the ethnic cleansing to which she was accustomed and of her surprise that he did not appear to be driven by it. She was engaged by his truthfulness and his sense of groundedness in a gracious reality beyond her well and bucket.

The profound listening of Jesus, in the Samaritan woman's experience, echoes in her comment to others who lived in her city: He "told me everything I have ever done!" (John 4:29). Listening, as in this story, does not mean not speaking or expressing convictions. Jesus did both. It does mean being open to the otherness of people who are seeking love, belonging, and meaning in their particular context. Listening is a self-giving for the sake of the other.

Eugene Peterson writes of the ministry of small talk, the discipline of being engaged by the ordinary. He writes, "Art is involved here. Art means that we give ourselves to the encounter, to the occasion, not condescendingly and not grudgingly but creatively. We're not trying to make something happen but to be a part of what is happening—without being in control of it and without it being up to the dignity of our office."[33] He observes that if Christian people are always manipulating conversation to talk about the big issues and the urgencies of our times, they are treating other people's ordinary as subspiritual.

In conversation that resists entering into the small talk and the ordinary of every day, we are like the disciples preventing the children from coming to Jesus, supposing that they are not worthy of his attention. Peterson puts it this way: "I don't think it is stretching things to see Jesus—who embraced little children, which so surprised and scandalized his followers—also embracing our little conversations."[34]

The emerging mission frontier calls for new dimensions of following Jesus. Jesus calls us to enact his identification with people as they are and where they are. The temptation to care with ulterior motives is staggering. Who can resist it? Only discipleship that follows the promptings of the Spirit will be able to rid the waters of our piranhas. Only that kind of discipleship will enable us to share in Jesus' listening.[35]

A contemplative style of evangelization and formation must grow out of attention to Jesus, who accepts us and all persons. Fred Kaan's hymn expresses the deeper dimensions of our identification with one another through Christ:

> Let your acceptance change us, so that we may be moved
> in living situations to do the truth in love;
> to practice your acceptance, until we know by heart
> the table of forgiveness and laughter's healing art.

Lord, for today's encounters with all who are in need,
who hunger for acceptance, for righteousness and bread,
we need new eyes for seeing, new hands for holding on;
renew us with your Spirit; Lord, free us, make us one![36]
("Help Us Accept Each Other," *UMH*, 560, stanzas 3, 4)

To be one with the stranger, with the foreignness in the seeker, is to be part of Jesus' reaching out and receiving persons as they are. Jesus is the primary practitioner of prayerful listening. In this light, congregations become mission outposts when they are sent out to listen to others with Christ.

Again, the emphasis upon listening is crucial because our aim is not to convince people to join in our activities and to support our institutions and programs. Our aim, our essential ministry, is to care for people at the deeper level of their longings for God and for a way of life that is hopeful and just. Our aim is conversion at deep levels. Unless we listen prayerfully, we will only touch the surface of people who are seeking God.

God's word is like rain coming down upon the soil (Isaiah 55:10-11). The rain comes down and brings forth fruit. That is God's part and God's promise. Our essential ministry is to let the rain, the Word of God, seep down to the deepest levels in people's lives and bring forth conversion. Listening allows us to hear people give us the signs that tell us where they are dry and thirsting. Then we can prayerfully and joyfully share with them the richness of the Word of God and the ways of faith and prayer.

How could your congregation more effectively follow Jesus in this way of listening? What change in priorities is needed to more fully care for people in Christ's name? What do people in your church need in order to begin to make connections with ministry to others in daily life?

The proposal is this: Leaders must envision a congregation that has "For God so loved the world" written on the genetic code of every member. What would it mean for you and other leaders in your congregation to shift the logic of ministry from protecting and caring for the ninety-nine (a gospel for insiders) to the logic of the ninety-nine finding the one (believers with a gospel for seekers)? Clearly, it would require a shift of focus and a recovery of the ministry of all the baptized.

## ESSENTIAL MINISTRY AS THE FLOW OF GOD'S GRACE

When we think in terms of the pattern of the congregation's essential ministry, our focus shifts the perspective from impersonal structures and functions to the flow of God's power and gracious Word. The pattern and spirit of this ministry looks beyond the organizational chart to the flow of God's transforming grace at work in the lives of people. On first reading, the tendency is to identify reaching out with evangelism, and helping people to find God with worship, and nurturing them in discipleship with Christian education. Successive reflection leads to a deeper reading. Distinct functions give way to an intuitive, organic movement. The flow of essential ministry reflects the interrelated qualities of God's preventing, convincing, converting, sanctifying, and perfecting grace.

Like a car that is badly out of tune, a congregation can sputter and move along with jerking, fitful lurches, each functional area moving along without a clear vision. By contrast, a congregation can move with a grace that resembles a galloping thoroughbred. The determinative reality is whether or not the congregation discovers and yields to the movement of God's grace in its basic ministry.

A congregation with a vision of reaching out to persons, welcoming and listening to them, relating with them to God, nurturing them in faith and prayer, and sending them out to live as disciples in the world will manifest the marks of a living organism, a finely tuned and highly coordinated body. The outgoing and compassionate movement of this body is a manifestation of the risen Christ living in the community of faith.

Where this gracious and outreaching ministry is not happening, congregational leaders must help the people see a vision of themselves as participants in the grace of God at work in daily life. Many congregations have become accustomed to an organizational model in which people choose pieces of the church's ministry, functional areas that they will do for three years or until they quit. The tasks supplant the faces of people. The vision of the wholeness of God's mission gets lost. Churches do not know why there is so little joy, yet continue faithfully to do their duty.

All the leaders, especially pastors, will need to provide spiritual leadership that will reorient the congregation to the work of the Spirit of God. So many congregations are burdened by the sense that they must do God's work for God, while the Spirit of Jesus hammers on the doors of the church asking to be admitted. Leaders, yielding to a deeper knowing in prayer and contemplation, are called to hear and help the people to receive Jesus, who sweeps away all the disconnected pieces and brings a rushing wind of freedom, and to join him in listening to people as seekers after God.

To use another image, the flow of grace moves like a river. Grace respects the channel as long as the channel does not restrict the movement of grace. If there is resistance, grace will cut a new channel. In this sense, the grace of God will always be subversive of our blindness and our narrow agendas. Jesus Christ, flowing in attentiveness to all persons, cuts through the bureaucratic mazes that oppose his sovereign freedom. The straight path to love's ocean will finally win. The flow of God's mission in Christ moves from the source to its destination with the force of divine gravity.

God's mission is not focused on the comfort and status of professional church leaders. Neither is grace generated by programs and activities, though grace *may* use them. Pastoral leadership is significant, and programs can be important, but only if they serve and release the joy and the vision of the congregation as God's mission outpost.

## GOD'S STORY AND OURS

God has a story. As biblical people, we have been telling and rehearsing this story for centuries. We say: "God's story is recorded in the Bible. We know it because we read it, sing it, study it, and act it out." This is the old, old story we love to hear, tell, and celebrate.

This is the recorded part of the story. There is more to God's story, which is being recorded in the bodies and journeys of people in all times and places. As some like to say: "We are writing Acts 29." That may be a bit sanguine, yet it makes a point. In and through the church, God continues to act and new chapters are being written. Yet such a view is far too narrow. God's story is not restricted to the faith community.

John Wesley preached God's universal grace. More than grace available for all people, he proclaimed that God's dynamic grace is working in the life of every human being, and God is acting in each moment to open the way for response to God's grace. The hopeful and encouraging teaching of universal and prevenient grace could be summed up in the affirmation that God is always ahead of us, anticipating our every move, always making a way for us to respond to God's offer of life in Christ.

Like the father in the story of the prodigal son (Luke 15:11-32), God is always waiting and looking for each person to come home. Like the prodigal's father, God is actively looking down the road. The astounding truth, if congregations will receive it, is that God will use our eyes and hearts to look and to care. Through our enactment of acceptance, forgiveness, joy, and guidance, people can respond to God and enter into life eternal in the here and now in daily life with the people of God.

In our essential ministry, we see that God's prevenient grace is already there before we meet a person. God is already drawing them, removing obstacles, and opening blind eyes.

The flow of God's story is woven into the story of every person. When Augustine of Hippo prayed, "Thou hast made us for thyself, and we are restless until we find our rest in Thee," he was saying that in our hopes, hurts, yearnings, dreams, will-to-live, longing to love and to be loved, God sets our course toward home. Even if persons should never find home, the story of every person bears within it a longing for home because God is longing with that person for home. Even if people do not know they are looking for home in God, God's prevenient grace is shaping the journey toward home and keeping the possibility open.

People who are drawn to the mystery of God and faith have a story to tell. When they sense that you are willing to listen, they will likely tell you their story. Many people have never had the opportunity to tell another person about their journey in life. If a setting is created for telling of the journey they have made and are making, they will begin to see and know with their hearts. In making their untold story a shared story, they begin to discover the connections and to see how God has been working to draw straight their crooked lines (prevenient grace). At the same time, they will want to know the listener's story: your story.

When someone enters our world with compassion and attentiveness, we want to know how they came into our world. It is so natural to ask the person who has listened to us, "Who are you? Where did you come from? What are you about?" At that moment, the conversation turns a corner and the listener has an opportunity to tell the stories of his or her journey and quest for faith. Each of us can see our reflection in the other and marvel at what God has been doing.

Our essential ministry as God's people is not to give people a book of doctrine or lectures on how to turn their lives around. We have ourselves to give in listening, caring, and faithful discipleship. We have the story of God as we have come to know it in worship and in Christian living. We can give people a chosen people who know the story of how they have been chosen. We can offer to others a welcome that says there is room for more.

What does all of this do? There are no certain results. Some people will look for a while and leave. Some will stay and move into a growing awareness of a transcendent voice sounding in their ears and of a hunger to hear the transforming Word of God. In God's time and in theirs, the stories may converge at the waters of baptism with the outpouring of the Spirit and a voice saying, "You are my child. Today, I have begotten you."

This might seem like a good place to end, but this is not the end of the story. On the other side of the waters is a life of vocation in the world which continues the course of the outreaching of Jesus' own ministry. The never-tiring stream of God's grace moves out in discipleship that continues to focus on people, reaching out, welcoming, listening, and relating with them to God through the Word and the waters of the baptismal covenant.

The story of God in the lives of Christian people moves outward continuously, drawing another and then another, into the stream that makes glad the city of God. The uncommon privilege of your congregation is to share in the transforming mission of God. Congregations and their leaders must keep this larger sense of God's mission in view as they engage in particular ministries and service.

## MINISTRIES OF CHRISTIAN INITIATION

There are a variety of roles and ministries that support people in the process of becoming Christian. Each of the roles described on this and the following pages play a part in surrounding seekers, hearers, and candidates for baptism with care, encouragement, support, and instruction as they move along the journey of conversion and initiation. Each is dependent in a special way on the grace of God that sustains the whole. The roles are briefly described so that you will have a sense of the basic responsibilities and relationships of each to the others.[37] Terms in parentheses are suggested as alternative designations for the ministries described.

**The Congregation:** Initiating persons into life in Christ is the responsibility of all of the baptized. All are called to share their faith and discipleship; to welcome seekers with hospitality; and to actively participate in worship, including the special celebrations that relate to persons in the process of Christian initiation. The congregation offers its witness and support throughout the initiation process. Chapter Seven will suggest ways that the congregation can prepare to be a welcoming and initiating people.

Each congregation has within it persons whose discipleship and spiritual gifts are recognized. They may or may not hold key elected positions, but they are persons who can serve as reliable and consistent guides in the faith journey. Persons who are seasoned disciples through mutual oversight, and in small groups, will be important in ministries that help inquirers, hearers, and candidates grow toward baptismal faith. For example, class leaders, persons in Covenant Discipleship groups or

Emmaus Walk reunion groups, people who have completed one or more courses of *Disciple* Bible study, and persons involved in other disciplined groups may be prospects for serving as sponsors and catechists.

**Sponsors:** The sponsor is a person who comes to know the inquirers, hearers, and candidates through regular contact during the formation process which begins with inquiry and continues through initiation and beyond. Sponsors witness the growing faith and transformation taking place in the person they sponsor. They keep regular contact with those they sponsor, in both informal conversation and in formational group sessions. They encourage persons who are seeking; listen to their faith and doubts; introduce them to others in the congregation; testify to their progress and accompany them in the services of Welcome, Calling to Baptism, and Baptism. Sponsors serve to offer genuine interest in the welfare of inquirers, hearers, and candidates. They normally assume their role throughout the full progression of the stages and services of Christian initiation. The care and ministry of the congregation for participants is most fully borne by the sponsors.

Sponsors may be the persons who initially reached out and welcomed the seeker into the inquiry stage. Or they may be assigned to this work. Sponsors are most effective when they are open, friendly, easy to talk to and be with, deeply rooted in the life of the congregation, and in their continuously growing relationship with God.

The sponsor may also be a godparent to a candidate. The difference is related to the duration of the relationship. Godparents establish a life-long spiritual relationship with the candidate and serve through faithful encouragement and guidance from baptism onward. Candidates may have both a sponsor and a godparent. Each sponsor should have a copy of *Accompanying the Journey: A Handbook for Sponsors*, published by Discipleship Resources. This book gives further details about the work of the sponsor.

**Catechist (Formation Director ):** One or more persons of sufficient maturity in the Christian faith and life serve as reliable guides through the stages of formation and instruction. The ancient church called them *catechists*, a term that comes from the Greek root *echo*. In a sense they are the resident hearing aids, for those seeking God. This suggests the peculiar nature of the guiding work. The Word is to be so internalized in the hearers and candidates that it echoes in both their thought and conduct. Catechists are able to guide, to listen, and to question in ways that evoke continuing growth and searching. They are able to help others hear the Word because they understand and practice hearing and obeying God's word.

In the early Methodist movement, their counterpart was the class leader who guided, corrected, reproved, exhorted, and loved those who had "a desire to flee from the wrath to come, and to be saved from their sins." (*The United Methodist Book of Discipline*, 1992, "The General Rules," ¶67, page 72)

The catechists lead regular formational group sessions. They understand the process of initiation with enough clarity to be able to guide the preparation of inquirers, hearers, and candidates through the successive stages and services. They take an active and visible role in the services of Christian initiation. The formational group sessions they lead consist of two parts:

◀ a time for formation in discipleship through listening for God's Word in the Scripture texts used in worship and in daily life experience;

◀ a time for responding to questions and concerns that emerge within the group (for example: use of the hymnal, an overview of the Bible's contents and organization, the establishment of patterns of prayer in the family, the basics of worship, the congregation's organization, reflection on the Lord's Prayer and the Apostles' Creed).

The primary focus or elements around which guidance and reflection take place are the congregation's worship, Scripture, prayer, and ministry in daily life.

Note: In this resource, the catechist is generally referred to in the singular, since most congregations will only need one. In congregations in which there are many persons on the conversion journey and a number of catechetical groups, the congregation may need more than one.

Each catechist should have a copy of *Echoing the Word: The Ministry of Catechists*, published by Discipleship Resources. This book provides guidance, interpretation, and direction for those who serve as catechists.

***Pastor(s):*** The primary role of the pastor is to receive and articulate the vision of welcoming seekers and making disciples. (For a further elaboration of the visioning work of the pastor, see *Quest for Quality in the Church*, by Ezra Earl Jones, published by Discipleship Resources.) When this is done faithfully and effectively, the pastor frees the congregation to become a mission outpost and to adopt Christian initiation as a basic structure of the congregation's ministry. The pastor must not state a vision arbitrarily or from on high. The pastor stands among the people—all of the people—in the congregation and in the community. There, listening to the longings of the people and listening to the Good Shepherd, the pastor casts a vision of the congregation engaged in its essential ministry.

When the congregation has decided to put Christian initiation in place as an essential structure, the pastor leads the congregation in the care of persons who are seeking, hearing, and preparing for baptism and serves as guide and shepherd to the sponsors and to the catechist. The pastor needs to be thoroughly familiar with the purpose and processes of Christian initiation and ready to affirm and support the congregation in the work of making disciples through its stages and services.

***Bishops and District Superintendents:*** In continuity with the historic task of the superintendent, bishops are entrusted with the responsibility of ordering the life of the church so that it is able to worship and evangelize faithfully. Bishops facilitate the initiation of structures and processes that equip Christian people for service in the church and in the world in the name of Jesus Christ (see *The United Methodist Book of Discipline, 1992*, ¶501). Bishops, in their office and leadership, along with the District Superintendents, link all the baptized to one another and to Christ, the head of the church.

This resource does not claim a particular episcopal role in regard to Christian initiation. The fact remains, however, that as bishops teach the centrality of the baptismal covenant in making, forming, and sending disciples, they empower pastors to give clear leadership in fulfilling the church's essential ministry. While the primary focus of this resource is on initiation processes in the local congregation, the leadership of the bishop and superintendents of an annual conference will significantly enhance the resources and the cumulative energy of pastors and congregations who will recover the adult *catechumenate* as a structure for evangelization, formation, and incorporation.

*Coordinator:* Though the position of coordinator is optional, a congregation may decide that the logistics of effectively implementing and supporting Christian initiation requires a coordinator. The coordinator, working with the pastor and catechist, enlists and coordinates the congregation's work in preparing persons for the services of the baptismal covenant and the other stages and services. Whether or not a church has a coordinator, those who lead the processes of Christian initiation must work as a team for the sake of the work of the whole congregation.

*Worship Director:* The worship director plans and brings necessary resources to the liturgical celebrations that mark the transitions between the stages of Christian initiation. The worship director may or may not have a visible role in these services.

*Musician:* The musician provides leadership in planning and coordinating music for the worship services of initiation. Normally, the musician is the same person that leads the congregation's total music ministry. If not, the musician related to Christian initiation will need to work closely with the congregation's music leader. See the Resource List at the back of this volume for musical resources for Christian initiation.

*Hospitality Director (s):* The church may choose to appoint a hospitality director who will attend to the physical and emotional comforts of the candidates. He or she embodies the Martha Ministry of the congregation.[38] When a welcome can be anticipated, the host will see that the congregation expresses tangible attention and hospitality. Arranging room space, appropriate heating or cooling, child care, transportation, refreshments, towels and baptismal garments, and a score of other matters, fall in this servant's care. In most situations, one person could not and should not do this work. Members of the congregation should be enlisted to take a hand in the work of hospitality as a way of enacting their promises and prayers for the candidates.

Every congregation will need to adapt these roles and ministries into a configuration that suits its ways of implementing Christian initiation. Congregations that are already engaged in an ongoing process can be extremely helpful in answering questions[39].

## ORGANIZATION AND TRANSFORMATION

A word of caution: as soon as we begin to assign roles, describe ministries, and organize for service, we tend to think it all depends on us. We sometimes think our work is as good as accomplished once we have enlisted persons and organized them to work toward a goal. The truth is that when we think this way we may be resisting, with premature and short-sighted closure, God's transforming power. In reality, what we have done is only to set the stage for collaboration with the power and presence of God already at work in the lives of those who are seeking God.

Transformation requires profound vision and deep trust in God's grace working in the lives of people who are beyond our control. Augustine's word points to the needed balance of grace and effort in the ministry of transformation: "Without us, God will not. Without God, we cannot." Keep the discipline of remembering that you are participating in God's mission as you welcome seekers and form disciples.

---

### BASIC CONCEPTS IN CHAPTER FOUR

❧ Leaders and congregations who seek to implement Christian initiation as an expression of their essential ministry should be clear about the choice, its risks, and its demands.

❧ There is an essential difference between membership orientation and Christian initiation. Membership orientation is usually aligned with an institutional agenda, rather than with an ecclesial foundation in God's mission. Christian initiation is aligned with the transforming power of God, working in people who long for God's new creation, which is offered in Christ and claimed in baptism.

❧ Ministry in a missionary context follows Jesus in its identification with people in their yearnings and struggles. Listening is an essential part of Jesus' ministry to people.

❧ The flow of God's grace is what affects conversion and calls forth our hospitality to those whose journey in faith moves them toward home. Processes, leadership roles, and functional tasks become important within the context of the movement of God's grace.

❧ While Christian initiation is the responsibility of the whole congregation, there are particular roles and ministries that welcome seekers and make disciples.

❧ Openness to God's transforming power, not our organization, is primary.

Chapter Five

# APPROACHES AND SETTINGS

*Eli said to Samuel, "Go, lie down; and if he calls you, you shall say,*
*'Speak, Lord, for your servant is listening.'"*
*1 Samuel 3:9*

God's gracious call comes to people with or without the church's action. The church's ministry is one of discerning God's initiative in the lives of people and guiding them as they learn to respond. Our work is to provide settings in which people can know God and practice listening and heeding the voice of God in Christ.

First Samuel 3 is a delightful story that illustrates this interplay of divine initiative and human agency in spiritual formation. All was quiet in the sanctuary at Shiloh. Eli, the old priest, was soundly asleep in his room. Samuel was sleeping in the dim light of the sanctuary near the ark of the covenant. During the night God called, "Samuel! Samuel!" Samuel heard a voice calling him, but he "did not yet know the Lord, and the word of the Lord had not yet been revealed to him" (1 Samuel 3:7).

For Samuel, the voice calling in the night could only be Eli's voice; so he answered the old man, "Here I am, for you called me." Eli knew that he had not called to him. When the scene played again, "Eli perceived that the Lord was calling the boy." So he told Samuel how to respond if the voice came again: "If he [God] calls you, you shall say, 'Speak, Lord, for your servant is listening" (1 Samuel 13:9).

God did call again. And Samuel, instructed in how to respond, answered the Lord, "Speak, for your servant is listening" (1 Samuel 13:10). From this powerful moment, Samuel grew to be one of the great leaders of Israel. Samuel's relationship with Eli and the worship of the people served as the setting for spiritual awakening, formation, discernment, and decision.

Every congregation must, if it is to fulfill its essential ministry, give itself to serve seekers and candidates as Eli served Samuel in the story. Christian initiation is an intentional process for helping people to know God and the Word of the Lord with an immediacy that frees them to follow Christ in daily life. In this chapter, we will consider the basic approaches and settings used in Christian initiation.

APPROACHES

❧ experience followed by reflection

❧ discernment

SETTINGS

- ◄ formational groups
- ◄ worship shaped by the Christian calendar and lectionary
- ◄ ministry in daily life
- ◄ ministry to the poor
- ◄ prayer

ADAPTATIONS

- ◄ for baptized seekers
- ◄ for parents and sponsors who are seeking baptism for infants and children

## 1. APPROACH: FOLLOWED BY EXPERIENCE AND REFLECTION

With the emergence of print technologies, Western culture quietly accepted the priority of understanding over experience. Western culture and the Enlightenment have highly prized the perceptual and conceptual powers of the mind and the use of cognitive processes. Much of the educational endeavor in schools, universities, and the church has favored learning about prior to or instead of learning by and in and with. More than likely, you have come through educational systems that relied on textbooks and curriculum plans that assumed you could master a subject objectively. In a real sense, however, this style of learning has been favored in place of another, more primary style: learning through experience.[40]

There has been a growing shift in educational philosophy since the 1960's. Educators have been rediscovering the power of direct experience to engage persons at many levels. For example, the Slingerland method allows children to use large muscle activities to discover the feel and shape of letters and numbers. Concern for the learner's ability to act and live responsibly in the real world of daily life has brought the theory of mathematics down to earth; students learn to balance a checkbook.

There is an urgency in the church to recover a sense of primary modes of learning. We are rediscovering that Christian transformation is not accomplished by teachers, guiding students through a curriculum in a printed quarterly, but by faith practitioners leading learners on the journey of conversion from birth to death.

*Come to the Waters* offers a method and worship resources in which experience is primary. The pedagogical method is one of experience followed by reflection. The learning journey invites persons to hear the Word in Scripture, to engage in ministry, to receive the sign of the cross on the forehead, to hear the Lord's Prayer, to experience the water of baptism and the laying on of hands, and to share the bread and cup at the Lord's Table, and so to discover the connections to what God is doing in daily life. Following each experience, seekers are invited to reflect upon it. Cyril of Jerusalem in his *Baptismal Catechesis* said to the neophytes:

> It has long been my wish, true-born and long-desired children of the Church, to discourse with you upon these spiritual, heavenly, mysteries. On the principle, however, that seeing is believing, I delayed until the present occasion, calculating that after what

you saw on that night I should find you a readier audience now when I am to be your
guide to the brighter and more fragrant meadows of this second Eden.[41]

Restraint in explaining services or discussing what will happen is urged. Sponsors
and catechists who are well prepared for their ministry will be able to support and
guide their candidates during the services without explaining everything beforehand.

Nothing about the services or any other aspect of Christian initiation is secret. If
candidates have questions, answer them. Answers should be appropriate to the
development of the person at that stage. The inquirer's need is determinative; not our
need to control or expound on various topics.

At the core of this approach to pedagogy is the experience of the church with
Jesus Christ. The witness of the Bible is that from the Garden of Eden to the Red Sea
to the meal in Emmaus to the wind and fire of Pentecost, human beings have experienced the call and claim of God. The role of the congregation and its various ministries with inquirers, hearers, and candidates is like that of Eli with Samuel.

Turning to that story again, we can now discern another facet of the way Eli col-
laborated with God in the formation of Samuel. Eli experienced a sleepless night
with the young Samuel, who had heard someone calling his name. Instead of
explaining, Eli, who discerned that the Lord was calling the boy, guided him to enter
more deeply into the experience: "Go, lie down; and if he calls you, you shall say,
'Speak, Lord, for your servant is listening' " (1 Samuel 3:9). In the morning, Eli urged
Samuel to bear the experience responsibly and not to withhold it in fear. In this way,
Eli encouraged Samuel to experience and to obey the voice of God. Eli did not inter-
pose himself as a mediator.

Those on the journey are persons who are learning to hear the resounding voice
of God. The congregation, through the sponsors and catechist, serves God and the
candidates best in leading them to discover the "sounding in the ear" of Jesus, who
calls disciples to follow him. As a method, experience followed by reflection entrusts
to God the work of calling and cautions us against too quickly offering our list of
do's and don'ts or our indoctrination or our brand of political correctness. As congregation and leaders, our task is to encourage and support all the people who seek to
hear and know God.

The congregation, reaching out and receiving persons into the fellowship of disciples, has the privilege of inviting others to a deep hearing of God's call in Jesus
Christ. Storytelling, worshiping, doing the word in service to the poor and suffering,
discovering opportunities for service in daily life, and reflecting on Scripture are the
curriculum for learning to hear the distinctive voice to which disciples must first and
finally listen. Continuous reflection on Scripture and the experiences of prayer, worship, gifts for ministry, and ministry in daily life are at the heart of the formational
process of Christian initiation.

## 2. APPROACH: DISCERNMENT

When I was twelve and in another tradition, I was prepared for baptism by the
pastor. Part of the process leading to baptism included meeting with several of the
elders of the congregation, who asked me several questions about my faith and com-

mitment. All went well; I was baptized and admitted to membership. The process was fairly formal and, to some extent, routine. The feeling I have to this day was that I was questioned so that someone else could make the decision about whether it was appropriate for me to be baptized and admitted to membership in the church.

A few years later, I attended membership classes in a Methodist congregation. I attended six classes and was received as a member with no questions asked! As far as I know, all involved assumed that attending the class moved automatically to becoming a member.

Christian initiation and the decision to move by stages on a journey of conversion and to arrive at last at the waters of baptism or reaffirmation of the baptismal covenant rely on mutual discernment. The approach is neither automatic nor one-sided.

Discernment is rooted in the same dynamic that is at the core of the whole process: God's calling and prompting and persons' listening and responding as conversion brings inner awareness to public celebration. Sponsors, with the help of the catechist, listen and encourage the pilgrims as they experience the voice of Jesus calling, "Follow me." This is a spiritual process that requires developing intuitive skills and growing confidence in our ability to interpret what we hear within us and experience in our lives. The services, with introduction and commentary, in Part Two point out the issues for mutual discernment.

## 3. SETTING: FORMATIONAL GROUPS

The journey of conversion is an accompanied journey. Climbing a mountain is best done by people in groups. When people travel together they learn to trust one another. When one wants to turn back, the others can remind him or her that the group is in this together. When one falls, the pitons and ropes of the others insure his or her safety and the possibility of continuing to the summit. Small groups are an essential element of Christian initiation.

For much of its history, the Methodist movement recovered the genius of this prudential means of grace. Many African-American, Fijian, and Korean congregations have maintained it to this day. The class meeting, at its best, is a means of sanctifying grace: people watch over one another in love to enact both the form and the power of godliness and to help each other to work out their salvation. (See *The United Methodist Book of Discipline, 1992*, p. 71, ¶ 67.)

Formational groups harness this expression of the means of grace and introduce seekers to it from the beginning of their journey. The groups meet weekly. They are made up of persons in the various stages of the process, their sponsors, and the catechist who leads the group. The groups provide the face-to-face environment needed for the faith development of the candidates. These groups meet throughout the process from inquiry to the affirmation of ministry. However, the duration of the process will be determined, not by whether the person has attended a prescribed number of classes, but by whether he or she has discovered and evidenced the truth of the conversion journey.

The catechist and sponsors uphold and represent for the candidates the faith of the whole church. They serve as the coaches and spiritual friends. They reflect with them on their experience of encountering the Word in worship, prayer, and service.

More will be said about the dynamics and content of the groups. At this point it is sufficient to say that the group meetings are a response to the Word encountered in worship each week and to the experience of life brought into that encounter. The flow of the sessions is a simple movement of

¶ prayer;

¶ reflection on Scripture and experience;

¶ appropriate preparation for the next service in the process of conversion;

¶ guidance for spiritual discipline and participation in the life of the church.

For one approach to the group, see the Appendix 1, p. 154.

The congregation supports these smaller communities of growing faith with prayers, weekly welcome to the hearing of the Word, a living witness to the ongoing process of being transformed through Word and sacrament, and service. The congregation trusts and obeys the Holy Spirit, who breathes life into those on the journey.

## 4. SETTING: WORSHIP SHAPED BY THE CHRISTIAN CALENDAR AND LECTIONARY

Christian initiation builds on both the services of the baptismal covenant and on the powerful drama of worship shaped by the calendar of the Christian year and the lectionary. See *The United Methodist Book of Worship* for the calendar and the lectionary and for worship services based on them. Worship prepared with these resources can be powerfully formative for the community of faith and those being initiated into it.

The calendar of the Christian year and the lectionary evolved as the script for celebration and outreach. Though the lectionary and calendar have changed significantly over time, they were developed in relationship to the catechumenate. As churches in areas such as Jerusalem, Antioch, Alexandria, and Rome proclaimed the good news to those who were drawn to its life in Christ, the church developed a calendar of celebration and of readings that told the story. These resources emerged as tools for winning and forming Christian disciples.

In this drama of salvation, Easter came to be the climactic moment in the formational process, as the catechumens were brought to the waters of baptism to participate in Christ's dying and rising. Lent was the intensive phase of preparation leading up to the celebration of the Easter mystery. In the Great Fifty Days, which followed Easter the church celebrated the fullness of life with the newly baptized, and together they entered more fully into the mystery and meaning of the Word and table. The Lent-Easter-Pentecost cycle was not merely a convenient way for the church to celebrate its faith; it was the primary way for congregations to proclaim their faith. It was worship evangelism.

In the Revised Common Lectionary (UMBOW, 227-237), the Scripture texts and particularly the gospel texts during Lent (Year A) serve to lead the people into a deep encounter with the reality of the living Lord. During the Great Fifty Days, the texts from Acts and the gospels call all to a fresh discovery of the missionary church living by the power of the Spirit.

In this process, the candidates for baptism have a peculiar ministry within the congregation. They are the focus of the congregation's attention and prayer; and as the Scriptures are proclaimed and the gospel is celebrated, the risen Christ uses those being converted to call the whole congregation to renewed and continuing conversion. In this way the church is built up together with those the Lord is adding to the community.

In one congregation, a candidate came to the moment of baptism and decided not to be baptized because, as she said, "I am not ready to die for Christ." Imagine the impact such integrity had on the congregation. A year later, the same person had grown so that she felt she was ready to yield all for the sake of Christ; and she was baptized.

## 5. SETTING: MINISTRY IN DAILY LIFE

Wayne Schwab, former evangelism executive for the Episcopal Church, takes a down-to-earth approach to the ministry of the baptized. It can be summarized as follows:

1. All persons are created to be in ministry or service. God created all persons to love and work, that is, to companion and tend the garden (Genesis 2). All persons are created, to do justice, and to love kindness, and to walk humbly with God (Micah 6:8). That persons are created to be in ministry belongs to the order of creation.

2. How we love and work belongs to the order of redemption. Those who are baptized into Christ are called to "walk just as he walked" (1 John 2:6). A primary aim in spiritual formation is to help people make the connection between daily life and faith. Formation during Christian initiation ought to help the auto mechanic, the stock broker, the sales person, and the student see their ministry

   ☞ at home with family (relationships and management of the home)

   ☞ at work (paid or non-paid)

   ☞ in the community (local political entities)

   ☞ in relationship to public issues (county, state, nation, world)

   ☞ in leisure time

   ☞ in the faith community

For many who are being drawn to faith and conversion, one or more of these areas of daily life will be places of struggle, the place where their current story is unfolding. Christian initiation is not about removing seekers and candidates from their daily lives. Rather it is about helping them to make the connections between what God is doing and what they are doing.

From the beginning of their relationship with seekers, sponsors and the catechist will help them to make connections by focusing on simple questions like these:

- Who is there? (in each of the six areas)

- What is going on?

- What is needed?

- Where do you see God at work?

- What do you do well?

- Who affirms your giftedness?

Inviting those on the journey to reflect on questions like these opens the way for telling their stories and celebrating their ministries in daily life. Rather than asking people to tell the story of a spiritual experience, this approach to storytelling connects concretely with their daily lives and invites them to link discipleship and faith in Christ with the relationships and places of their everyday world.

This is not to imply that talking about transcendent experience, such as Samuel's call in the night or Mary's encounter with Gabriel, is not proper for the conversion journey. Spiritual experiences should be welcomed and discussed. The discipline of focusing on ministry in daily life will serve to make clear both the context and the connections discussed.

In light of the faith journey, it is important to say that this is not simply an issue for Christian initiation. Accountability for ministry in daily life—reviewing, affirming, forming, and celebrating the ministry of every baptized member—is an ongoing task of the congregation. Those who move from inquiry at the first to affirmation of ministry at the end of the process must then be supported continuously throughout their lives. Covenant Discipleship groups or Emmaus Reunion groups are two specific forms of ongoing support for ministry in everyday life. Your congregation's strength in forming new disciples is directly linked to the consistency with which it nurtures and supports disciples in their daily-life ministry.

Preaching, prayers in worship, formational groups, informal discussion in growing relationships, personal reflection in silence and in a journal will be strengthened by an ongoing attentiveness to ministry in daily life. Leaders in the process, along with all in the faith community, can and need to move forward the sense of ministry in daily life. Deeds need to be illuminated and announced when possible. The ministry of children, youth, retired persons, women, and men can be celebrated regularly as witness to the promptings of the Spirit of God at work in all of the people. A new business, a new home, adoption of a child, a marriage, acceptance of a vocation, retirement, election to a public office, a new job can all be celebrated and affirmed as opportunities for ministry and as points at which persons are listening to the One who calls us to follow.

Leaders have responsibility for helping the congregation be aware of ways of viewing Christian existence in the world. Helping people to see the ways the systems around them affect their lives and the lives of others will deepen their understanding of the nuances of God's call in daily life and in the broader dimensions of Christian stewardship.

Making disciples means struggling with ways of making decisions and establishing values. It means asking questions: Is it biblical? How do others see it? How do Christians see it? What does my inner light, the witness of the Holy Spirit, teach me? Guiding disciples to decide, to offer it to God, and to pray as a way of moving through the days and weeks is teaching practical discipleship. Meeting to talk about choices and decisions is one of the ways we offer them to God and sharpen our mutual ministry.

## 6. SETTING: MINISTRY WITH THE POOR AND MARGINALIZED

The ministry of the baptized in daily life has a complement in the ministry of the congregation as the body of Christ. Formation in a life that becomes the gospel cannot evade Jesus' call to attend to the poor. The focus of Jesus' own life and ministry was given largely to those who were on the margins of the economic and social structures of his day. He preached good news to the poor, and he was good news to the poor. Doing acts of justice and compassion in the context of the congregation's ongoing witness and service engages candidates in an encounter with Jesus, who identifies himself with those in need (Matthew 25:31-46).

Leaders will need to discern the appropriateness of inviting inquirers, hearers, and candidates and their readiness to share in the congregation's work for justice and compassion among the poor and suffering.

The word *poor* may be an uncomfortable word for you. Many people are more comfortable with focusing ministry on peace with justice, systemic change, and social justice. There is, however, a concreteness about poverty and the grinding suffering, violence, exclusion, and hunger of the poor that makes it more personal and more immediately urgent than more abstract language about justice and peace.[42]

Christian social teaching and conversation about God's preferential option for the poor expresses God's attentiveness to the concrete reality of persons excluded by the forces of oppression at work in society. Poverty is not only a collective social phenomenon; it is a real and daily experience that denies God's justice and compassion to real people whom God loves. John Wesley's ministry focused on the marginalized; and the Methodist Societies related to the poor, imprisoned, and excluded.

Christian initiation, as learning to hear the voice of Jesus, engages those who are becoming disciples in the congregation's ministry to and with the needy. It invites a fresh hearing of Jesus in the hungry, the sick, the lonely, who are often made invisible by their social, economic, and racial-ethnic exclusion from the wealth, status, and power of the culture.

Most congregations already have in place ministries to and with the poor. Christian initiation calls them to engage hearers in these ministries as a part of the process of formation and conversion. Ministries to the poor are opportunities for candidates to participate in concrete acts of justice and compassion that embody God's good news. In this way, the congregation invites each person to know firsthand the meaning of one of the questions that will be asked at baptism: "Do you accept the freedom and power God gives you to resist evil, injustice, and oppression in whatever forms they present themselves?" (*UMH*, p. 34, number 4)

Leaders should seek to engage those on the journey in the congregation's ministries with the poor and suffering and to reflect with them on the experience of encountering human need in the context of hearing the Word of God. Sponsors and the catechist will seek to bring this dimension of the journey into dialogue with the other elements of Christian initiation: Scripture, prayer, and worship.

One word of caution: There is a difference between a particular social agenda and the flow of God's grace. The temptation to use the candidates for our social agenda, however just and compassionate it appears to us, may place leaders in the role of being piranhas. As in all of the processes of initiation, discernment of readiness is critical. Jesus threw down the gauntlet to people who hesitated to follow him (see Luke 57-62). Leaders exercising discernment will know when to urge the next step and when to wait and let the gospel do its deeper preparation beneath the surface. The goal in formation is always to support the church's young Samuels as they hear and respond to the Word of God.

## 7. SETTINGS: PRAYER

Prayer is a part of all of the approaches and settings we have outlined. Like young Samuel, those who are being formed and initiated should be surrounded with the attentive and watchful prayers of the congregation. There are specific times of prayer and praise in the services of welcome and calling to baptism, in the weeks of intensive preparation, at baptism, and in the weeks that follow. Throughout the journey, sponsors pray for and with their apprentices in faith. Catechists guide the congregation and formational groups in prayers that anticipate the coming day of baptism and the growing wisdom, faithfulness, and discipleship of each candidate.

In a real sense, Christian initiation is a school of prayer as a way of life. Prayer is experienced and learned in its many forms and postures: corporate praise, liturgical prayer, private prayer, silence and solitude, meditation, prayers of reflection on the Scriptures and on seeing one's self in the story, and prayer response to the needs of others. In the process, prayer becomes the crucible in which daily life and the life of the faith community are connected in the hearts and choices of the candidates. In the next chapter, we will consider in more depth the formation of Christian affections and the religion of the heart.

## 8. ADAPTATIONS

Christian initiation introduces a change of paradigm for the way the church collaborates with God in making new Christians. As discussed in Chapter One, the emerging mission frontier suggests that we take seriously adult conversion. Inviting adult seekers to journey with you and to come to the waters of baptism is the basic process explored in this resource. However, as Chapter Three points out, there are many people with circumstances that do not fit the model of unbaptized adults. Since God's grace is not limited to one process, the congregation and its leaders need to be skillful in adapting the process to those in other circumstances. Part Two will elaborate the two basic adaptations of the process. For now, a brief description of these adaptations will suffice.

### a. Adaptation for baptized seekers

Youth and adults who have already been baptized may also be seekers who need to participate in a journey that brings them to a deeper experience of faith and a return to the baptismal covenant. Unlike candidates for baptism, baptized seekers are already members of the household of faith. Some may have been baptized as infants, but did not subsequently receive formation and nurture in faith appropriate to their development. Others may have been only sporadically involved in the faith community. Still others may have been confirmed in adolescence, but now find themselves immersed in a deeper experience that cries out for God, new life, and reaffirmation of what was given in baptism.

The general rule of thumb with baptized seekers is that the congregation and its leaders will affirm their baptism and welcome their participation as members of the body of Christ. Rather than including them in the prayers for the candidates for baptism, the congregation should offer prayers for them that are appropriate to their search which leads to profession of faith in confirmation or reaffirmation of the baptismal covenant. As far as the formational groups are concerned, baptized seekers may be included if that seems best in congregations with small numbers of seekers. When there are large numbers of baptized seekers, it may be best for candidates for baptism and those seeking to reaffirm the baptismal covenant to meet separately.

Because they are already baptized, the services for candidates for baptism are not appropriate for them. The resources in "Services for Persons Returning to the Baptismal Covenant" in Part Two pertain to these persons.

### b. Adaptation for parents and sponsors seeking baptism for infants and children

The church affirms the appropriateness of baptism of persons of any age, including infants and children. In addition, the church strongly encourages the preparation and formation of the families of those who are unable to answer for themselves at baptism.

In the emerging missionary context, the congregation cannot assume that parents seeking to bring their children for baptism are both willing and able to guide them toward a profession of faith and a life of discipleship. Most parents need much of the same welcome and preparation that youth and adults preparing for baptism need. Some parents may, in fact, be simultaneously preparing for their own baptism or reaffirmation as they prepare to bring a child for baptism.

"Services for the Initiation of Children," with introduction and commentary, in Part Two give direction for the congregation's ministry with a parent or parents who are inquiring about presentation of a child for baptism.

BASIC CONCEPTS OF CHAPTER FIVE

❧ Our work as congregations is to provide settings in which people can know God and experience listening to and heeding the voice of God in Christ.

❧ The approaches and settings for Christian initiation include these:

- Experience followed by reflection is the consistent learning approach in the process.

- Mutual discernment of need and readiness is at the heart of the formation process.

- Worship shaped by the liturgical calendar and the lectionary serve as a basic setting in which both the congregation and candidates for baptism are formed.

- Formational groups meet weekly so that the process is an accompanied journey.

- Ministry in daily life grounds discipleship in the world.

- The congregation's ministry among the poor and oppressed connects pilgrims to corporate service.

- Prayer permeates the process and is the crucible where faith and discipleship in everyday life are integrated.

❧ Adaptations of the basic pattern include consideration of

- adults and youth who have been previously baptized. Part Two provides appropriate services, with introduction and commentary, for the previously baptized.

- parents inquiring about presentation of a child for baptism. In a missionary context, the ministry of welcoming and preparing parents for the baptism of a child engages them in evangelization and formation prior to the child's initiation. Part Two contains appropriate services, with introduction and commentary.

# Chapter One

Chapter Six

# THE CALENDAR AND THE LECTIONARY

T he drama of the gospel of Jesus Christ structures the way Christians keep time.[43] The ancient missionary church embraced Jesus' distinctive story as the basis for its calendar of remembering and celebrating. The crucifixion and resurrection of Jesus was the center-point of all Christian celebration and worship.[44] In time, the Church added another cycle, which focused on the incarnation of the eternal Word in Jesus. Christians today keep time using two great cycles: the cycle of light, with Christmas-Epiphany at its center, and the cycle of life, with Good Friday-Easter at its center. The gospel stories form the calendar and serve as the content for the calendar's cycle of celebrations and remembrances. Rather than being a burden of observance, the Christian calendar was and is an evangelical tool for proclaiming Christ as Savior and Lord, and for calling people to conversion.

## THE CHRISTIAN YEAR AND MISSIONARY CONGREGATIONS

Without the story of God in Christ rooted in time and events and without texts that tell the story, there can be no shape to the Christian life, worship, and outreach. Christian discipleship is shaped by the push of the biblical tradition and by the pull of the contemporary situation. Forming and initiating Christian disciples must be deeply rooted in remembering and celebrating the ways God has acted in the history of Israel and in Jesus Christ. Without this, Christianity becomes a set of rules to live by or a philosophy divorced from the action and mission of the triune God. Without this deep remembering and celebrative rehearsal in worship, the church lacks content and develops amnesia. The current recovery and widespread use of the calendar of the Christian year and of the lectionary as its companion tool is a sign that Christians want to remember the rock from which they are hewn.

When the church celebrates the biblical Word and the sacramental deed, it is doing what William Willimon calls "think-thank." The Greek word is *anamnesis (an-am-né-sis)*. Anamnesis is the opposite of amnesia. In our rapidly changing post-modern culture, Christians are continuously on the edge of forgetting who they are. The antidote for amnesia is gathering for worshiping remembering, rehearsing, and thanking God for all that God has done in Christ from creation until Christ's coming again in glory. In the weekly celebration of God's deliverance in Christ, all who participate find that Jesus Christ is their contemporary. The opening greeting of the service of Word and Table combines anticipation and proclamation of the presence of Christ:

> The grace of the Lord Jesus Christ be with you.
> **And also with you.**
> The risen Christ is with us.
> **Praise the Lord!**[45]

When we, the worshiping community, gather in expectancy and experience the risen Christ, we welcome seekers and offer them the opportunity to share in our experience of the paschal mystery, our encounter with the crucified and risen Lord.

The calendar of the Christian year developed as a way of doing "think-thank" systematically. In this way congregations in Jerusalem in the third century, or North Africa in the fourth century or Britain in the fifth century, could retell their story, telling it to people who came into the life of faith from pagan backgrounds. A Spanish pilgrim named Egeria tells of the dramatic worship of the church in Jerusalem late in the fourth century.[46] She describes street processions to holy places, crowds singing psalms, pilgrims praying and praising God as they recalled Jesus' passion at Golgotha, holy awe as they moved to the empty tomb. Pilgrims and seekers participated in the mystery and the drama of Jesus' passion and resurrection. They participated in the contemporary reenactment; through it, the power and grace of Christ's saving death and resurrection became a present reality for them. Over time, this vital evangelical practice was weakened as the church gained official recognition in the Roman empire. Per Harling summarizes the shift in Western Christian worship:[47]

- ❧ In earlier Christian churches, worship was something done in memory and in praise of the risen Christ.

- ❧ During the middle ages, worship became something said in memory and in praise of the risen Christ.

- ❧ During the Protestant Reformation, worship became something heard (and understood) in memory and in praise of the risen Christ.

Doing, saying, and hearing are essential in vital worship and evangelism; but communal action (doing) is essential if the whole person and all the people are to be drawn into worship and conversion that transforms them, through encounter with the living Christ.

Christian initiation and the revised services in the hymnals and books of worship of most denominations signal and invite a recovery of worship as something done by the whole congregation. This is a dramatic shift and one that requires courageous and loving leadership on the part of pastors, musicians, and other leaders.

Conversion and faith are nurtured by remembrance and praise rooted in God's story with which we are joined in baptism (Romans 6:3-11). The calendar and the lectionary were developed as tools of missionary communities surrounded by cultures that did not know the story. The calendar and lectionary became basic resources for ongoing conversion and building faith both for believers and for seekers. Many present day congregations are discovering the transforming power of worship as a rehearsal of God's mighty acts of salvation.[48]

Christian initiation is the way the church lives and incorporates people seeking

God. By use of the calendar of the Christian year and the lectionary, congregations engage in "a lifelong and ever deepening spiral of Gospel-conversion-baptism-eucharist-mission."[49] In this ever-deepening spiral, believers are continuously renewed in faith and seekers are drawn into the dramatic action of God's grace. Worship is a living catechism.

## THE REVISED COMMON LECTIONARY
## AS A SOURCE FOR PREACHING, INSTRUCTION, AND FORMATION

A lectionary is a table of readings that follows the outline of the Christian year. The *Revised Common Lectionary,* published in 1992, is both a calendar and a table of suggested Scripture readings for a three-year cycle.[50] The readings for each Sunday and holy day provide a systematic approach to the use of Scripture in worship and assure a broad use of biblical material in relation to the celebration of the central mystery of our faith: the life, death, and resurrection of Jesus Christ.

The use of a lectionary is not the only way congregations plan for reading Scripture in worship. Some follow a modified use of the lectionary for part of the year, for example, during Advent-Christmas and Lent-Easter; and during the rest of the year, they follow another plan. Some churches follow a plan of reading and preaching the books of the Bible over a period of weeks or months. The recovery and widespread use of the lectionary by United Methodist congregations points to its value in helping congregations hear the whole message of the Bible.

In this resource, we strongly recommend the use of the Christian calendar and the lectionary as sound and tested resources for planning worship, preaching, instruction, and formation of disciples. For those congregations and pastors who choose to follow another approach, more will be said at the end of this chapter.

The four basic components in the processes of conversion and formation of disciples—worship, Scripture reflection, prayer, and ministry in daily life—find their focus and content in the lectionary texts (see Figure 1). The approach to formation and instruction is experience followed by reflection. The continuing cycle of experience and reflection is informed and given substance by the calendar and the lectionary's systematic approach to encounter with Jesus. The inclusion of Old Testament texts and other New Testament texts broadens the gospel texts by providing a context in which to understand them. However, the focus of Christian worship centers on an evangelical-sacramental encounter with Jesus as the source and summit of salvation and grace for daily discipleship.

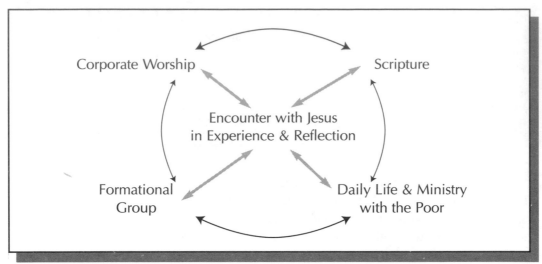

**Fig. 1**

These elements and their relationship with one another are more fully discussed in the previous chapter.

## THE THEMES OF LENT

Since Lent, Easter, and the Great Fifty Days developed as times of formation for new Christians, they are at the heart of the processes of Christian initiation. The lectionary readings and prayers of the church during Lent are especially suited to the quest of those seeking baptism. Later in this chapter, we will provide a brief outline for adaptation of the basic pattern to the Advent, Christmas, Baptism of the Lord, and Transfiguration cycle. Your congregation may decide to use both cycles as periods of time for inviting people to come to the waters of baptism.

The earlier stages of Christian initiation (inquiry and formation, see pp. 34-35) lead into conversion and a service of calling the hearers to baptism. The Scripture readings for the Sundays of Lent support intensive preparation of candidates for baptism and engage Christians in spiritual preparation for the renewal of their baptismal vows. Further, Lent is a time when Christians who have lived outside of the communion of the church, called returning members (penitents in the ancient church), are restored and reconciled to life in the faith community. "Invitation to the Observation of Lenten Discipline" states:

Dear brothers and sisters in Christ:
　　the early Christians observed with great devotion
　　　　the days of our Lord's passion and resurrection,
and it became the custom of the Church that before the Easter celebration
　　there should be a forty-day season of spiritual preparation [for the faithful].
During this season converts to the faith [catechumens]
　　were prepared for Holy Baptism.

It was also at this time when persons who had committed serious sins
    and had separated themselves from the community of faith [the penitents]
        were reconciled by penitence and forgiveness,
        and restored to participation in the life of the Church.
In this way the whole congregation was reminded
    of the mercy and forgiveness proclaimed in the gospel of Jesus Christ
        and the need we all have to renew our faith.
I invite you, therefore, in the name of the Church,
    to observe a holy Lent:
    by self-examination and repentance;
    by prayer, fasting, and self-denial;
    and by reading and meditating on God's Holy Word.[51]

*(UMBOW, 322)*

In this traditional text, we see how Lent is viewed as a communal journey in which the faithful, the catechumens, and the penitents are invited to make their pilgrimage to the cross and to Easter.

What follows is a brief focus on the themes of the lectionary texts in relation to processes of Christian initiation and conversion. In a time when the church is seeking to recover its roots and identity in scriptural understandings of baptism, the lectionary texts offer a short course in the meaning of baptism as a powerful and gracious encounter with Jesus Christ.[52] Preachers, catechists, worship planners, musicians, and sponsors should be alert to the kinds of connections made between the text and the baptismal covenant service.

Before characterizing the readings for each of the three years, consider the following general comments about the Lenten lectionary texts, their emerging themes, and the deepening formation and preparation of candidates for baptism.

- The readings for Lent, Years A, B, C, are found in *The United Methodist Book of Worship*, 230-231.

- The three readings for each Sunday are closely related to each other and keyed to the gospel reading.

- The readings focus on conversion.

- The Scripture readings during Lent are primary catechesis for candidates for baptism. The readings for Years A and B open up the service of baptism. The readings for Year C explore five great themes of baptism.

- There are clear and important links between the readings and the sacraments of initiation (baptism, laying on of hands, and Communion).

- These texts are common resources for the catechist, sponsors, preachers, musicians, and worship planners as they walk with persons through the initiation processes in Lent and Holy Week.

- Since experience precedes reflection in Christian initiation, the text of the baptismal covenant service is for the leader's own reflection in directing and leading the candidates. The candidates' primary engagement should be with the

Scriptures. By contrast, during the Great Fifty Days which follow baptism at Easter, the newly baptized will appropriately reflect on the experience of the sacraments of baptism, laying on of hands, the Eucharist, and on the texts of those services.

### The progression of the first five Sundays in Lent, year A[53]

1. We turn away from evil. (Matthew 4:1-11)

2. We turn toward Jesus Christ. (John 3:1-17)

3-4. We confess that we thirst for Jesus and the work of God in our lives. (John 4:5-42 and John 9:1-41)

5. We enter into death, putting our whole trust in Jesus Christ who is "the resurrection and the life." (John 11: 1-45)

All of the gospel readings are powerful encounters with Jesus, the Word of God. The gospel readings are drawn from Matthew and the great initiation texts of John 3, 4, 9, and 11.

The other readings are closely linked to the theme of the gospel readings. The first readings during Lent, Year A, are chosen to illuminate the gospel and are great narratives of the struggle of faith. The second readings are from Romans with one exception.

### The progression of the first five Sundays in Lent, Year B

As in Year A, the first Sundays in Lent, Year B, can be seen as a movement through the service of baptism.

1. We turn away from evil. (Mark 1:9-15)

2. We turn toward Jesus Christ. (Mark 8:31-38)

3-4. We confess that we thirst for Jesus and the work of God in our lives. (John 2:13-22 and John 3:14-21)

5. We enter into death, putting our whole trust in Jesus Christ who is "the resurrection and the life." (John 12:20-33)

The focus is on the Gospel of Mark and readings from John 2, 3, and 12 respectively. The first readings are chosen to illuminate the gospel readings. The second readings come from five different New Testament letters.

### The progression of the first five Sundays of Lent, Year C

The readings for the first five Sundays invite exploration of the great themes of baptism.

1. By a confession of faith, we are oriented to the triune God and empowered to resist evil and to live in gratitude. (Luke 4:1-13)

2. In Christ's death and resurrection and through baptism, God makes a saving covenant with us; and we say "Yes" to the baptismal covenant and to reaffirming it throughout our lives. (Luke 13:31-35)

3. In conversion and in baptism, Christ calls us to renounce evil and to accept the freedom to resist evil, injustice, and oppression, in order to serve him. (Luke 13:1-9)

4. Holy Communion is the feast of Christians, the renewal of our covenant with God, food for the journey, our sacrament of unity, and a foretaste of the reign of God. (Luke 15:1-3,11b-32)

5. In baptism, Christ calls us to a new identity. Former values, pursuits, investments, and habits pass away so that knowing and serving the living Lord may be our chief and defining goal. (John 12:1-8)

Though the focus is on the Gospel of Luke, the fifth Sunday's Gospel text is from John 12. The first readings are chosen to illuminate the gospel readings and come from both narrative and prophetic passages. The second readings are chosen from five different New Testament epistles.

God works in both congregation and candidates to build and to shape faith as the leaders and the people prayerfully prepare for the exploration and application of the Scripture readings during Lent. The themes listed here are not suggested as a preaching or worship planning program. Rather, they point to the relationship and flow of the texts with respect to the anticipation of baptism at Easter. The themes may inform planners and preachers and catechists, but the shape and depth of encounter with Jesus should be experienced in dialogue with the Scripture texts themselves. Let the Gospel texts witness to and invite encounter with Jesus.

## EXAMINATION OF LIFE AND PREPARATION FOR EASTER

### A. Anticipating the depth of conversion

Perhaps the significance of the readings and the themes will be clearer if seen not only in the context of worship, but in the context of transformation, which the Spirit seeks to work in the hearts of candidates during the period of intensive preparation for baptism. At baptism, adult candidates will be asked about the depth of their conversion:

❧ Do you renounce the spiritual forces of wickedness, reject the evil power of this world, and repent of your sin?

❧ Do you accept the freedom and power God gives you to resist evil, injustice, and oppression in whatever forms they present themselves?

❧ Do you confess Jesus Christ as your Savior, put your whole trust in his grace, and promise to serve him as your Lord, in union with the church which Christ has opened to people of all ages, nations, and races?" (*UMH, Service of the Baptismal Covenant I*, p. 34, No. 4).

No one can fully comprehend the depth of those questions or the meaning of a positive response for the rest of his or her life. What we can be clear about is that the candidates have made an accompanied journey in order to cross a line that changes their identity and loyalty forever. Romans 6 says that in baptism, each candidate will stand on the edge of the grave and affirm a readiness and a desire to die to sin and the power of evil and to be raised to a new life of trust and service in the name of One who is both Savior and Lord.

From the time of their calling to baptism on the first Sunday in Lent, candidates anticipate these questions that are at the heart of conversion and initiation into the life of the church. The congregation promises to love and pray for them during the weeks leading to baptism. Sponsors are given the charge to "support them in keeping disciplines of prayer, fasting, meditation on the Word of God, and examination of conscience." (See item 4 in "A Service for Calling Persons to Baptism" on p. 114.)

The meaning of salvation, new birth, and conversion is not limited to forensic transactions and acquittal at the judge's bench. As blessed as pardon is for sinners, they can bear good fruit only when they are grafted onto a good root (John 15:1-11). Faith can never stop at belief in *what Christ has done*; it must always anticipate what Christ stands ready to do in the hearts that welcome him and yield to his love. Salvation and conversion are profound transformations in and of the human heart, of the deep sources of our passions, affections, and desires from which those actions and choices arise.

Put bluntly: To implement the structures of Christian initiation in the congregation without aiming for a profound reordering of the heart is to miss the dynamic grace of the gospel of Jesus Christ. The examination of conscience raises the issue of our understanding of the goal of faith and the means of grace.

### B. Examining the heart and recovering the image of God

Examination of conscience is more than looking for wrongdoing or character flaws and dredging up guilt. What is at stake is the heart's affections, desires, thirsts, and passions (pride, avarice, anger, fear, self-will, love of the world, unbelief) that are contrary to the love of God and love of neighbor. Each of us has these within us, and they cling to our actions and choices; so we have lost our capacity to reflect the image of God. This examination of the heart aims at a self-awareness that is prepared to die with Christ and to be raised to newness of life that bears God's image. The aim is not heroic self-correction and willed conversion unassisted by grace. The aim is a living community gathered around Christ and steeped in the means of grace so that believers and seekers grow continuously in knowing their sin, in repenting of their disordered affections, in having faith in God, and in beholding the love of God so that the heart and its affections are changed by seeing God in love and worship. The transformative principle is this: What has our attention, has us. So anchored in love, peace, joy, and the other fruits of the Spirit (Galatians 5: 22-23), the affections are transformed to whatever dispositions are holy (Wesley's sermon, "The Way of the Kingdom," II.1, 12, 13). Such a transformation is the essence of the religion of the heart. It does not have so much to do with understanding (the mind) as it does with ordering the affections of the heart in relationship to God and neighbor. Wesley saw that good fruit could be born only by a plant grafted onto a good root. This grafting took place through faith in the ever-blessed Trinity, whose glory created us and pours the love of God into our hearts for our brothers and sisters. So filled and beholding God, we are changed to God's likeness, from glory into glory, by the Spirit of the Lord ("The Way of the Kingdom," II:12).

### C. Examination of the heart during worship and formation groups

There is a critical side to examination that we call repentance. Repentance begins when we see ourselves as we are: our need, brokenness, unexamined complicity with injustice, unconscious alliances with the evil powers of this world, thirst, blindness, and death. Christ is victor over sin and death. The candidates and the faithful can only know how great is their deliverance if they know the scope of their enslavement to sin, the powers of evil, and death.

The early church practiced rites called scrutinies on the third, fourth, and fifth Sundays in Lent. The community, using exorcisms, sought to cleanse the candidates of unclean spirits. In modern initiation rites, the purpose is to lead the candidates in self-searching and repentance by uncovering in the heart and memory what is weak, defective, or sinful and to strengthen what is strong and good. Rather than the community and its leaders examining the conscience or exorcising evil, the candidates scrutinize themselves during times of silence while the community prays for them. (See the section on "Examination of Conscience" in Part Two, p. 117.)

During Lent and Holy Week, the texts of the lectionary invite the candidates and the faithful to stand in the light of Christ where they can see their temptations, weakness, desires, blindness, and death and where they know their need of Christ as Savior and Lord. With Nicodemus, the woman at the well, the man born blind, Lazarus, Mary and Martha, candidates are drawn into encounter with Jesus, the deliverer.

The lectionary texts, combined with skillful and compassionate direction from sponsors and the catechist, will help the candidates to stand in the purifying light of Christ. The point here is that preparation for baptism is not a checklist of faults to be rid of, as much as it is a process of collaboration with God's Spirit in revealing both the truth of who the candidates are and the truth of who Jesus is. The encounter with Jesus in the gospel narratives during Holy Week is startling in its contrasts: Christ's faithfulness and our capacity for fickleness, Christ's courage and our betrayal, Christ's forgiveness and our self-justification, Christ's glory and our slowness to believe.

The pastor, sponsors, and catechist are called to lead in this process of experience and reflection that prepares the candidates for entrance into discipleship through baptism, the laying on of hands, and the Eucharist. The goal may seem to load the congregation with an overwhelming responsibility for repentance and conversion of the heart and will. The more accurate and gracious truth is this: When the means of grace are faithfully used, God can be trusted to do what God intends to do both in the candidates and in the faith community. The congregation and those who represent it to the candidates are called to faith and discipline no less than the candidates themselves. The results will build up the candidates and the faith community.

## HOLY WEEK AND THE GREAT FIFTY DAYS
## AS INTENSIVE SPIRITUAL FORMATION

With the start of Lent, the candidates for baptism enter into the congregation's continuous search for deeper conversion. Liturgically speaking, this process culminates in the church's participation in the drama of Holy Week, Easter, and the Great Fifty Days.[54] The depth and intensity of the people's reliving and rehearsing Jesus' passion, death, resurrection, ascension, and the outpouring of the Holy Spirit will have a powerful and profound impact on the candidates. Holy Week can be seen and experienced as the congregation's week-long retreat with the candidates and their sponsors. If not the whole week, then Holy Thursday through Holy Saturday can be observed in this way. Those who have experienced the Walk to Emmaus or Cursillo will have some idea of the power and the strong sense of community that develop during a journey with Christ.

As you plan for Holy Week, Easter, and the Great Fifty Days, consider the following services as settings where conversion and faith formation can be nurtured and supported in the context of a congregational journey:

### ☙ **Holy Week**:

- Passion/Palm Sunday (*UMBOW*, 338-343)

- Daily Services, Monday through Thursday (*UMBOW*, 343-349). *The New Handbook of the Christian Year* (pages 152-158) offers orders of worship.

- Holy Thursday Evening (*UMBOW*, 351-354). This is the night on which returning members are restored and reconciled to the church.

- Service of Tenebrae (*UMBOW*, 354-361). [See Part Two, "Services for Persons Returning to the Baptismal Covenant," pp. 138-150.]

- A Service for Good Friday (*UMBOW*, 362-365).

- Other acts of worship including The Way of the Cross and Holy Saturday (*UMBOW*, 365-367).

### ☙ **Easter Season**

- Easter Vigil or the First Service of Easter (*UMBOW*, 368-376). This is the night when candidates are baptized and the members of the congregation reaffirm their baptismal vows. Easter Vigil is the primordial service of all Christian worship. Plan this service well.

- Easter Vespers. *The New Handbook of the Christian Year* (pages 214-218) offers resources that give special honor to those baptized at the Easter Vigil.

- Resources for worship during the Great Fifty Days (*UMBOW*, 377-400).

- Ascension Day (*UMBOW*, 401-404).

- The Day of Pentecost (*UMBOW,* 405-408).

- An Order for Commitment to Christian Service (*UMBOW*, 591-592) is a strong resource for affirmation of vocation in daily life and is recommended for use in the service on the Day of Pentecost.

*The New Handbook of the Christian Year* provides expanded commentary on all of these services and is recommended as a supplement for planning worship during Lent, Holy Week, Easter, and the Great Fifty Days.

The point to be remembered throughout is this: Your congregation is not performing a passion play for the candidates. The congregation, as a faithful community, is living through the death and resurrection of Jesus. In welcoming and accompanying the candidates on the journey, all partake of an openness to God's transforming grace which is mediated through Scripture reading, remembrance, ritual enactment, and participation in God's mighty acts of salvation. Your congregation is not a bystander. It is the Easter community reliving its own birth and baptism. In doing this in faith and penitence, the congregation is the womb from which God begets new sons and daughters. In the Gelasian Sacramentary's service for presenting the gospels and for opening the ears of those enrolled for baptism, the presbyter says to the candidates: "And so the church, now pregnant with your conception, rejoices that in these festal rites she is in labor to bring forth new lives."[55]

In God's gracious economy, the candidates' journey toward new birth brings the congregation itself to the font from which it came, in repentance, conversion, and participation in the dying and rising of Christ.

Planning by leaders and broad participation on the part of the congregation is essential.

❧ Keep the schedule of church life, its worship and reflection, focused on the paschal mystery. Busyness should be set aside, not only during Lent, but during Holy Week and the weeks of Easter. Focus on the means of grace; on praise; on the mystery of participation in Christ's death and resurrection in the sacraments; and in ministry to the poor, the suffering, and oppressed.

❧ Keep action and drama in the foreground. Worship during Holy Week, Easter, and the Great Fifty Days is not so much didactic and cerebral as it is dramatic and participative. Trust the power of God, working in the gospel story, to evoke and order emotions, affections, and wills. For example, the reading of the passion story on Passion/Palm Sunday (see *UMBOW*, 340-342) brings the people down from the Mount of Olives to Golgotha. There is no need for further preaching in this service. Why preach about what the people have already experienced? The story read well and supported with congregational singing is a converting means of grace.

❧ Balance the personal and the corporate. As with all of discipleship, there is a need for personal reflection and experience balanced with corporate journey. Silence in worship, formational groups, church retreats, and other gatherings allow for the living Lord to speak both personally and corporately to the community of faith.

❧ Make creative use of the resources of the Book of Worship. (See *UMBOW*, 338-408.) Services for Lent and Easter evolved in the missionary context of the early church. Their purpose is to create settings where the converting Spirit is released to work in the faith community. While these services are largely complete, they invite appropriate adaptation to local needs, customs, and resources.

❧ Engage the people in planning, leading, and participating in worship and the other actions of this season. This is not a time for people to be spectators. The potential for conversion is directly related to the degree to which people see and experience themselves as contributors and participants in the drama of Christ's passion and resurrection. The wisdom of a Chinese proverb applies to worship: *What you hear, you will forget; what you see, you will remember; what you do, you will understand.*

❧ Keep in mind that the services of Holy Week are public events. Many visitors and seekers will join in the journey. If what they experience is vital and rich with God's hospitality to strangers, some will become inquirers and seekers, as the journey begins again.

## THE GREAT FIFTY DAYS

The vision and intention of Christian initiation is that the newly baptized will have experienced the sacraments and will have been included among the faithful: "You are a chosen race, a royal priesthood, a holy nation, God's own people, in order that you may proclaim the mighty acts of him who called you" (1 Peter 2:9). They will have experienced more than they can articulate or understand. The joyful worship of the congregation during the Great Fifty Days allows for an extended period of reflection on their new birth from above, their new life as God's own, and their participation in the priesthood of all believers in the ministry of daily life. The lectionary texts from Easter to Pentecost, as in the earlier stages of Christian initiation, give substance and focus to the maturing of God's new daughters and sons.

## CHRISTIAN INITIATION ADAPTED
## TO THE ADVENT–TRANSFIGURATION CYCLE

The calendar and lectionary for Advent, Christmas, the Baptism of the Lord, and the Sundays after Epiphany are a contrast to the Lent, Easter, Pentecost cycle. While the latter focuses on the past and the faithful memory (*anamnesis*) of Christ's passion, the former focuses on the future and the vision of the coming reign of God in the return of Christ. Lent, Easter, Pentecost focus on baptism as dying and rising with Christ. Advent, Christmas, Baptism of the Lord focus on baptism as new birth. Those who lead candidates for baptism through final preparation can use the calendar and the lectionary readings for the Advent-Christmas cycle as primary resources for worship, formational groups, and intensive preparation for baptism. The following progression outlines a way of adapting the process to the Christmas cycle:

❧ The inquiry stage begins any time persons are drawn to the good news of Christ.

- ¶ A Service for Welcoming Hearers can be used at any time during the year when the inquirer knows that he or she seeks Christ and the leaders sense that the inquirer is ready to move into the journey of conversion.

- ¶ The formation stage may be an extended period and has no specific tie to the calendar of the Christian year.

- ¶ A Service for Calling Persons to Baptism may take place on the first Sunday of Advent.

- ¶ The final preparation stage includes the weeks of Advent and Christmas.

- ¶ A service of the Baptismal Covenant may take place on the Sunday of the Baptism of the Lord.

- ¶ The integration stage during the remaining weeks after Epiphany or Baptism of the Lord, leads to Transfiguration Sunday.

- ¶ A Service for Affirmation of Ministry takes place on the Sunday of the Transfiguration of the Lord.

A careful reading of chapters Two and Five along with the commentary in Part Two of *Come to the Waters* will keep the focus on the essential process even though the calendar and lectionary texts illuminate the advent, incarnation or birth, baptism, ministry, and transfiguration of Jesus.

You may choose to use both major cycles of the calendar of the Christian year for accompanying candidates for baptism. This has the advantage of providing two times in the year in which candidates can be formed, initiated, and nurtured toward vocation in daily life.

## SCHEDULING BAPTISM:
## MOVING PAST BAPTISM AS A SERVICE RENDERED TO THE PUBLIC

Like most United Methodist congregations, yours may be accustomed to scheduling baptisms and reception of members at the convenience of individuals and their families. This is a vestige of an understanding of baptism as a service the church renders to the public. We encourage your congregation to work toward baptism at Easter, when the calendar, lectionary, and celebration of the central mystery of our faith converge and focus on Christ's passion and victory or at the Baptism of the Lord. (See *UMBOW*, 84, for additional appropriate days.) At first, such a shift will seem radical, and questions will be raised about the inconvenience it poses for people who want the expected service. Adequate preparation of the congregation must precede this new approach to scheduling baptism.

Chapter Seven will outline an approach for preparing the congregation for welcoming, forming, and baptizing as a basic structure of congregational life. Implementation of this approach will take time. If done with care and adequate formation of the congregation, scheduling baptism at particular times of the year will eventually be experienced as a natural expression of the Christian way of keeping time with Christ. The congregation will have new ways to be hospitable to people seeking baptism without succumbing to the get-it-done-when-they-want-it syndrome, on the one hand, or resorting to cold refusal, on the other. See the Introduction and Commentary to "Services for the Initiation of Children" p. 123 in Part Two.

## WHEN THE CONGREGATION FOLLOWS A PLAN OTHER THAN THE LECTIONARY AND CALENDAR

While Lent and Easter form the liturgical heart of the Christian initiation process, your congregation may decide, for pastoral reasons, to use the pattern described on pages 34-35 without following the calendar and the lectionary.

The pattern described in Chapter Two is adaptable. Those who decide to adapt the recommended use of calendar and lectionary will need to give careful consideration to the following:

1. *See that the Scripture readings used in worship proclaim Jesus Christ and invite encounter with him*

   ◆ as the one who calls and claims us as his disciples;

   ◆ as the one who invites us to share in the mystery of his dying and rising. The texts should be evocative enough to allow for in-depth reflection in the formational groups.

2. *Insure that worship preparation supports the journey of conversion with*

   ◆ appropriate celebrations of welcome into the processes of conversion;

   ◆ calling to baptism those who are ready;

   ◆ baptism;

   ◆ affirmation of vocation for ministry in daily life.

3. *Help seekers, hearers, and candidates to focus on the centrality of Jesus that leads to*

   ◆ baptismal union with him in the mystery of his death and resurrection;

   ◆ welcome of the gift of the Spirit who leads and prompts movement toward conversion;

   ◆ engagement in the ministry of the baptized as Christ's royal priesthood.

4. *Support candidates learning to practice the Christian life as followers of Jesus through*

   ◆ reflection on ministry in daily life;

   ◆ preaching and instruction that invites consistent and faithful use of the means of grace;

   ◆ patterns of congregational life that invite use of the means of grace in small group participation, in searching the Scriptures, and in accountability;

   ◆ guidance in use of the general means of grace—watching, self-denial, taking up the cross, exercising the presence of God—as means of persever-ance.[56]

---

BASIC CONCEPTS IN CHAPTER SIX

- ◆ The drama of the gospel of Jesus Christ is the structure of the church's way of keeping time with Christ. The dying and rising of Jesus is at the center of Christian worship.

- ◆ Stories from Scripture shape the calendar of the Christian year and serve as the content for the calendar's celebration and remembrance of God's saving action in Christ.

- ◆ The Christian calendar and lectionary developed as the churches tools in a missionary context.

- ◆ Conversion of the passions and affections, and faith in Christ are nurtured and ordered through ritual actions rooted in God's story and mission. The goal of preparation is a deep and thorough conversion, leading to the renunciation of evil and sin and the profession of faith in Christ as Savior and Lord.

- ◆ The lectionary texts for Lent and Holy Week, combined with the skillful and compassionate direction of leaders, help candidates stand in the light of Christ that leads to repentance.

- ◆ The process of the Lent-Easter-Pentecost cycle can be adapted to the Advent-Christmas-Transfiguration cycle or to an approach that does not use the calendar or the lectionary.

- ◆ A congregation with a strong understanding of baptism will find ways to initiate new Christians according to its way of keeping time with Christ.

# Chapter Seven

# PREPARING THE CONGREGATION

*"[Christian initiation] is not a 'program'—*
*it is the way the church is, the way the church lives."*
Robert Hovda[57]

Contemporary houses have front steps but no porch. Instead of porches, newer houses have decks at the back. Porches are structures that welcome. A porch says, "Come sit down. Rest a while. We can talk." By contrast decks are geared to privacy and exclusive gatherings. A porch is a vantage point where people observe and meet the passing world. Assorted chairs, hammocks, tables, and plants create an invitational environment where people can wonder and question. On the porch, neighbors can meet and talk, without going inside. Porches are in-between structures. Between the steps and the interior, the porch offers people a place to be. Porches allow for discovery and for testing relationships.

## PEOPLE ON THE PORCH

Congregations need a ministry structure that serves as a porch so that people who live in the house and people passing by can get to know each other. Without a porch, persons who do not know the life of faith may be rushed into the church without needed formation, or they will stagnate on the sidewalk. A porch is a place where seekers can experience unhurried time and unhurried relationships with the faith community, where they can participate in prayer and worship without being pushed to go in. It is a context in which they can test the reign of God. Without a porch, candidates may miss God's hospitality to strangers.

This chapter aims at encouraging your congregation to add to its ministry structures the porch of Christian initiation. Your congregation is a household of faith. As a people of faith, you live together in worship, service, study, and mutual care and oversight. Some of your people were born in the house, and it has always been home to them. Others came up the front steps because someone invited them. The steps represent all the ways the congregation invites and offers access to the household of faith.[58] Without steps, entry into the house would be steep and difficult. Advertisements in the yellow pages, the sign board in front of the church building, public events like choir concerts and ice cream socials, events for seekers, recovery groups that meet in the church building, clearly marked entrances to the church office, and personal witness to the Lord's transforming power all serve to signal that access to the congregation's life and resources is possible and hospitable.

However, for many people, steps that lead immediately to the door of the house can be threatening. When congregations have no porch between the steps and the interior of the house, there is no safe zone in which to test the Christian life and to explore life with Christian people. By contrast, a porch allows people a gracious, unthreatening space in which to say hello, tell stories, and sense what the people who live inside are like, how they think, and what really matters to them. Porches allow neighbors and passersby to climb the steps and try on your church and the gospel. Churches need porches.

Doug Murren and Mike Meeks, pastors at Eastside Church in Kirkland, Washington, clearly portray the need for a church porch: "[The unchurched] need a safe and often long preconversion stage in which they build confidence in us, establish the authority of Scripture, and cement relationships. We have to honor that phase. Unchurched people today distrust church, and they need to come and just watch us for a while."[59]

## STRUCTURES THAT SUPPORT CONVERSION

Chapter One introduced the three movements or structures of conversion and entrance into the life of the church. In a time when congregations must recover a missionary sense, in a culture that is largely indifferent or hostile to the gospel, steps and porches take on a much greater importance. During the first half of the twentieth century, the culture was viewed as basically Christian; the common assumption was that people were more or less Christian in thought and action. All that was needed was a decision to become a member of the congregation and to profess one's faith.

Things have changed in the last forty years. As your congregation approaches the twenty-first century, it will have to be conscious of evangelization (the steps), formation and instruction (the porch), and initiation into the sacraments (the front door into the house of faith). *The focus in this chapter is on the congregation's task of getting itself ready to offer formation and guidance to seekers.*

What follows is a proposal for the process of adding a porch to your church. The design of this process parallels the basic pattern of Christian initiation outlined in Chapter Three. To be more specific, this proposal is not so much for building a porch as it is spending several months on the porch so that your congregation knows that it has a porch and that the porch has a purpose.

## DECIDE TO SPEND SIX MONTHS IN CONGREGATIONAL FORMATION

If initiating persons into the life of discipleship through baptism is to be basic to the congregation's essential ministry, then people in the church need the experience of spending several months recapitulating and rehearsing the fullness of their own journey of conversion and initiation. People in your congregation are people of faith. They are people who deeply appreciate the hymns, worship, fellowship, and familiar patterns of doing things. They are churched people. Some can remember vivid experiences of faith formation and are conscious of and ready to share their deep love for God. However, many may have a less clear sense of their faith journey. They may not be able to articulate in words and images their journey before-Christ to after-Christ. This is not about blame or failure. Rather, it points to the need for a fuller welcoming of the gospel story told in the course of the church year, celebrated in the sacraments of baptism and the Lord's Supper, and enacted in daily life.

What this resource proposes is a major change in the way the congregation sees itself and its work. Change must be made with the deliberate support of the pastor and other leaders of the congregation. Since the whole congregation will be involved, it is important that a decision to spend several months on the porch be made with the support and understanding of the church council. Careful teaching and information need to be offered so that everyone understands that a significant congregational journey is about to take place.

The outline below suggests the stages and movements of a six- to nine-month pilgrimage. We assume that your leaders will invoke the Spirit to put flesh upon it and breathe life into it so that the congregation becomes a resurrection people transformed for its essential ministry of making disciples. Ideally, your congregation will begin this journey together in the Fall of the year so that it moves toward the climactic focus of Lent, Holy Week, Easter, and Pentecost. If your congregation chooses to work with a different time frame, make appropriate adjustments. (See Chapter Six.)

Often a product bears a caution on the label so that the consumer will know the risks and dangers of its use. Here is the caution that goes with your congregation's decision to spend time on the porch: Spending time on the porch is a major reorientation of the congregation to the central elements of Christian tradition:

- the centrality of the Scriptures read and reflected upon;

- the sacraments as primary means of grace;

- conversion shaped and supported by participation in worship and ritual action;

- the ministry of all the baptized;

- ongoing participation in small groups;

- life-long witness and service in the world;

- the means of grace as a way of living in relationship to God.

Embarking on this journey carries the risk and the promise of transformation for each member of the body of Christ and the congregation as a whole. The Holy One of Israel says,

> [My word] shall not return to me empty,
> but it shall accomplish that which I purpose,
> and succeed in the thing for which I sent it.
> Isaiah 55:11

If you and other leaders are convinced of the need for becoming a disciple-making congregation on the emerging missionary frontier, trust that God's word will be like rain on arid ground. Perhaps the image of your congregation's doing a rain dance sounds strange, but it might also suggest the kind of intense expectancy and prayer that are needed to launch church members into a fresh experience of their own conversion and baptism as Jesus' disciples.

## 1. TELL THE STORIES OF SPIRITUAL JOURNEY

Form small groups in which members of the congregation are invited to tell their stories. Many Christians have not experienced telling the stories of their quest for meaning, love, and faith. When people experience the hospitality of being listened to with compassion and attention, they experience the grace of Jesus, walking with them (see Luke 24:13-29); they discover that hopes and disappointments can be shared and that a new sense of being accompanied begins to grow.

These are approaches that may be used:

❧ Structure the conversation around the lectionary readings. Identify the stories of spiritual journey in the biblical texts and use them as a basis for asking questions about and exploring each person's journey in faith. Encourage and stimulate storytelling with questions like these:

- What are the major events or turning points in your life?
- What place do God and faith have in your life and how did you come to faith?
- What does it mean to hear and to follow the call of Jesus Christ? What does it mean that you have been baptized?
- Are you ready to reorder your life through worship, prayer, reflective study, and community life in order to hear and follow the call of God in Jesus Christ?

❧ Structure the conversation around the events of daily life and work. Read "Ministry in Daily Life" in Chapter Five as background for discussing the events of daily life and work. It will help people to take stock of the settings in which God is already working. During the small group meetings, encourage people to talk about home and friends, work, community, public issues, leisure time, and faith community. Ask questions such as these:

- Who is there?
- What is going on?
- What is needed?
- Where do you see God at work?

When people are invited to reflect on questions like these, they are encouraged to find ways to talk about their stories and to discern and affirm the ministry of each person in his or her daily life. Rather than asking people to tell the story of a spiritual experience, this approach to storytelling leads them to look at their daily lives and invites them to make the connections between faith and life that are the stuff of discipleship and faithful ministry in Christ's name. Many of the people in your congregation will welcome the affirmation and discovery that their lives matter to God and that the risen Lord is with them as they discern needs and opportunities to love God and neighbor.

❧ Structure the conversation around reading Scripture and discussing several basic questions. A simple and effective Bible study approach for small groups is to ask the group to read a text three times, alternating women and men's voices. After the first reading of the text, invite the participants to respond to the question, "What did this reading say to you about who God is?" After the second reading, ask "What did this reading say about who you are?" After the third reading of the same text, ask "What is the risen Lord prompting you to do?" While this may seem too simple, it has the strength of direct encounter with the text and practice in listening for the Word of God in reflection on Scripture. (See Appendix 1 for a variation of this approach.)

A word of caution: You may be tempted to use a study book for this process. That may be appropriate; but before using a study guide, be sure that it is not a means of avoiding the depth of each person's quest and story. If the threat of being vulnerable is an issue, train group leaders in some basic rules such as creating a group covenant that includes confidentiality and mutual affirmation, listening without judgment, and trusting in the Spirit of God to work in the group. Building trust and caring relationships is a basic part of this exploration.

As you plan for these groups, envision each person having an opportunity to tell about his or her search and to discover an openness to a continuing and thorough conversion. This time of storytelling should last six to ten weeks and is equally appropriate during the fall or the weeks from Advent to the Sunday after Epiphany.

During the same period, preach sermons in a narrative style in order to help the people experience the questions and the voices of the biblical figures who wrestled with hearing God, interpreting the meaning of events, shaping faith and conversion, and responding to Jesus' call in their daily life and work.

## 2. MAKE AN OPEN INVITATION TO A LENTEN JOURNEY

In the weeks prior to Lent, plan for preaching that will include an invitation to conversion and to a new beginning in faith. Focus proclamation on the call of Christ to follow him. Announce that those who desire to declare and celebrate a new beginning in faith will have an opportunity to enact this on the First Sunday in Lent.

Lent is a premier opportunity to experience conversion. Since the modern church has not experienced Christian initiation as a basic structure in congregational life, congregations have tended to view the Lenten observance as a time heavy with repentance and introspective discipline. We have overlooked the plain and ancient words of the "Invitation to the Observance of Lenten Discipline" in the Ash Wednesday Service: "During this season converts to the faith *were* prepared for Holy Baptism" (UMBOW, 322). The recovery of Christian initiation aims at making the statement in the present tense: During this season, converts to the faith *are* prepared for Holy Baptism. Many in your congregation will welcome the opportunity to rehearse and rediscover the converting grace of God during the congregation's Lenten journey.

### 3. CELEBRATE NEW BEGINNINGS
### IN FAITH ON THE FIRST SUNDAY IN LENT

After the sermon on the first Sunday in Lent, use "A Celebration of New Beginnings in Faith" (*UMBOW*, 588-590). Do not hurry this response to the Word. Public witness and the congregation's affirmation of that witness are part of renewal. Prayer and the laying on of hands may include making the cross on or over the person. Ritual enactment builds faith, engages persons in multisensory experience, and is a powerful force in shaping faith and life.

One additional consideration for this day: Assign spiritual friends or spiritual partners for those who decide to publicly celebrate a new beginning in faith. While these persons are not the same as the sponsors described earlier in this book, they can enact the faith community's concern for one another as they begin a new journey. Encourage these persons to support one another in conversation and prayer during Lent and Easter.

Continue or begin new groups that will meet weekly until the Day of Pentecost. Since Christian initiation employs four basic components in forming disciples—worship, Scripture reflection, prayer, and experience in ministry and service—encourage all of the groups to find ways to be engaged in the experience of and reflection on all four. Groups may take on some form of ministry to the poor and suffering. Group convenors can help each group to recall what most touched and shaped them in the previous Sunday's worship. Reflecting on one or more Bible texts, preferably texts used in the worship of the previous Sunday, should be a central component of each week's group meeting. Prayer in the group and privately will help participants to encounter the One who is present to us as we are open to others. In a noisy and busy world, the experience of silence can be both strange and refreshing.

### 4. FOCUS ON ENCOUNTER WITH CHRIST DURING LENT

Lent's intensive character is heightened by the gospel readings (especially in Year A). Plan for worship and groups to focus on the readings as encounters with Christ. While Lent does have its penitential side, the Sundays of Lent are to be celebrations of the risen Lord who meets us in Word and sacrament. Make full use of musicians and readers who have prepared carefully in order to heighten the dramatic impact of these encounters with Jesus. For example, discover the power of gospel readings with musical participation by the congregation. (Listen to David Haas's "The Samaritan Woman," "The Man Born Blind," and "The Raising of Lazarus" in *Who Calls You By Name: Music for Christian Initiation*, Volume II, Chicago: GIA, CS-257, which includes two audio tapes and a libretto).

Let worship be a powerful experience of Christ in Word and table. During these Sundays, Jesus is no slumping cross bearer. He is the one about whom every hearer must make a fresh assessment and response. This is not a season to focus on ourselves and our efforts; it is a season of journey in the company of One who is a mystery and a sign of God for us. Trust the gospel and the work of the Holy Spirit to work conversion in the people.

The focus of reflection during this stage is given to questions such as, "What must change (die) in me in order that God's new life might burst forth in my life? How will we live for God?" Invite attention to Jesus' calling us to fight evil and injustice and to become participants in the reign of God in the world. In Lent, the journey moves strongly into the experience of conversion that leads to saying *no* to evil in order to be free to say *yes* to Christ.

## 5. EXPLORE AND EMBRACE THE LORD'S PRAYER AND THE APOSTLES' CREED

*Gracious Voices: A Sourcebook for Christian Initiation*, edited by William P. McDonald (Discipleship Resources, 1997) has a substantial section on the Apostles' Creed and the Lord's Prayer. Make use of these readings in preaching and in small group reflection during the weeks of Lent. Include the Lord's Prayer and the Apostles' Creed in weekly worship in ways that move past the routine to a sense of vital engagement with the prayer and the faith of the church. One approach is to invite the congregation to sing one or both of them. Your church musicians should be able to help you find or create appropriate musical settings. Another approach is to hand over the faith and prayer of the church to different people each week. (See Part Two, pp. 116-117, where these actions are described.) Many Christians have not experienced a full and conscious participation in the faith and prayer of the church. Plan worship and study so that they have the opportunity to experience the drama of giving and receiving faith and prayer.

## 6. ENTER INTO THE MYSTERY OF DYING AND RISING WITH CHRIST

Holy Week and the Great Three Days (Holy Thursday, Good Friday, and Holy Saturday) are the liturgical crucible in which our faith in Christ is formed. During this time, the journey moves from the porch to the front door and into the house. In these eight days, Christians rehearse the story of dying and rising with Christ and celebrate the mystery of our baptism into Christ. *The United Methodist Book of Worship*, 336-376, provides the essential orders and instructions for leading the people into a full experience of "Remember your baptism and be thankful." No other period of the year is more intense or filled with the transforming power of the gospel.

Be courageous in planning and leading worship during this period. Pastors and other worship leaders are tempted to presume that people will not want to parade with palm leaves and banners on Passion/Palm Sunday or have their feet washed on Holy Thursday or stand around a bonfire on the eve of Easter. Some will not, yet many will be ready to participate in the dramatic movements of the liturgy of Holy Week and The Great Three Days. Remember: While many church members are used to worship that is oriented to speaking and to printed texts, seekers, unfamiliar with church ways, are hungry for experience, for drama and action. The gospel is inherently dramatic, and your congregation's journey for the sake of the world can develop ways of enacting the drama with grace and power. Expectancy, not fear or timidity, will allow you and others to stand aside so that God's grace is free to move in power through dramatic services of worship.

The Easter Vigil (*UMBOW*, 368-376) is the primordial service of all Christian worship. On this night the ancient church baptized new converts and renewed their own baptismal covenants. Initiating this service will be your congregation's discovery of the potency of full liturgical celebration. If you do not do anything else, do the Easter Vigil! Invite all the people to rejoice in the risen Lord, through fire, Word, water, and Eucharist. Liturgically speaking, Christian initiation's midpoint and pinnacle is the Easter Vigil. "This is the night when Jesus Christ broke the chains of death . . . and we are reconciled to you!" *(UMBOW, 372)*

Study the service fully and plan it well. Involve a team of leaders in planning the service so that it can be the work of the people. The Easter Vigil is not a service that a pastor or musician can plan or lead single-handedly.[60] Allow for dramatic and creative engagement with the biblical texts. Dull reading will anesthetize the people. Pull out the stops! Solemnity need not be boring or labored.

This night is a wonderful and most appropriate time for baptisms, confirmation, and personal or congregational reaffirmation of baptismal faith. The service of the baptismal covenant will be all the more powerful in light of the pilgrimage of continuing conversion that you and your church have been making over the preceding months.

## 7. LEAD IN EXPLORATION OF THE MEANING OF THE SACRAMENTS AND THE CALL TO JESUS' MINISTRY

The celebrations of the Great Fifty Days, centered on the readings from Acts and the gospel texts from John, open the way for exploring the mystery of our relationship with the risen Lord in the power of the Spirit. The readings of Scripture in worship and again in small groups are central to reflection on the sacraments and on our vocation as disciples.

Plan worship and small group reflection toward a deeper experience of the life and mission of the Church. Many of the people in your congregation may not have explored the mystery of union with the risen Lord in baptism or the mystery of touching the wounds of the living One in the Eucharist. The Luke 24 and John 21 texts on the third Sunday of Easter beg for reflection on the sacraments. The texts for the following Sundays focus on the Shepherd who leads us, the call to abide in Jesus and to bear fruit, the work of the Spirit in the disciples, and the unity of the church in the unity of God.

The sacraments have been neglected, trivialized, or underestimated in many congregations. The Sundays of Easter invite full-blown celebration of Word and table. This is a good time to test a weekly celebration of the Eucharist. Lead the people in reflecting on the experience of the sacraments.[61] Let the evangelical joy and the power of Easter shine forth in eucharistic celebration!

The Great Fifty Days invite discovery of how baptism and Eucharist are experienced as God's continuing call to ministry and witness in daily living. Keep worship, preaching, and small groups focused on questions like these: In the areas of your daily life and work, how is the Lord prompting you to see yourself in ministry? What is your special calling? What spiritual gifts have been discerned in you by this community? How will your life be offered as a living sacrifice in the community of Christ's priesthood and in the world?

The lectionary texts for the Sundays of Easter provide rich material for reflection on how the early community connected Easter faith with daily life and loving God and neighbor. Remember that children, the retired, those who are in various ways challenged physically or mentally, may need special support and affirmation for their ministry. Too often gifts and vocations are clericized with emphasis on church vocations and organizational roles. Resist narrowing the full work of all who belong to the baptismal covenant.

## 8. CELEBRATE DAILY-LIFE MINISTRY AND AFFIRM SPIRITUAL GIFTS ON THE DAY OF PENTECOST

Through the preceding experiences on the "porch," your congregation will have discovered the rich truth that all are in ministry. Pentecost is a day to celebrate that reality. Acts 2 is couched in the language of supernatural phenomena, yet the glory of God then and now is that people are amazed and astonished that ordinary Galileans (substitute your community's name) are able to declare in word and deed God's power. Prayer enacted in song, liturgy, and sermon can evoke a similar wonder at the mystery of God's loving and working through all of the people.

Following the sermon, invite those who are ready to embrace a particular ministry to come and stand before or among the congregation. The pastor or lay leader can ask, "Having determined to live out your baptismal covenant in daily witness and service, will you endeavor to follow Jesus Christ under the guidance of the Holy Spirit?"[62] Other questions may be asked about specific vocations and forms of witness or service. Offer prayer for those who have come forward. "An Order for Commitment to Christian Service" (UMBOW, 591-592) may be used as the structure for celebration and affirmation in this service. (See Part Two, p. 108 and pp. 120-121.)

Imagine yourself as the pastor, saying, "Dear friends, today we recognize the ministry of Cindy, Don, Hecter, Amanda, and Phil; and we commission them to their special tasks in the service of Jesus Christ. Phil has discerned that his work as an auto mechanic is service to Christ. Cindy and Don have come to recognize that they have a very special ministry in loving and teaching their children and in encouraging each other in their love and work. Amanda wants to be a voice for fairness and understanding in the way the community treats migrant workers. Hector has decided to run for the school board as a witness to God's care for the youth in our city. He also wants to serve as a sponsor for a person who is searching for God. Blessed be God, the giver of all good gifts!"

When your congregation has made its journey to the baptismal covenant, they will have experienced the kind of processes that they can offer to others seeking faith and eternal life. They will have discovered how good and gracious a porch can be, and they will be eager to spend some time on the porch with those God will send to them. Your congregation will be ready to prepare to invite and accompany others who are on the journey of conversion.

## BASIC CONCEPTS IN CHAPTER SEVEN

❧ Contemporary congregations need a structure that serves as a porch so that believers and seekers can get to know each other in the context of the transforming gospel of Jesus Christ.

❧ This is a major shift in the architecture of the congregation's ministry.

❧ In order to make this shift, the congregation needs an extended period of revisiting their tradition and experiencing their own journey of conversion and initiation.

❧ A six-to-nine-month pilgrimage that begins in the fall and moves through Advent, Lent, Easter, and Pentecost can begin to reorient the congregation so that its focus is not on program and activity but on the means of grace and on helping people discover their spiritual journey. This congregational journey will focus on the primary components of formation and making disciples: worship, reflection on Scripture, prayer, and ministry in daily life.

# PART TWO

*Services and Prayers for Christian Initiation*

# Notes for Part Two

*The following services and prayers assume that the user is familiar with Part One of this book, in which the principles and processes of Christian initiation are set forth. The services and prayers in Part Two form the hinges, the transitions, in the congregation's process of welcoming, forming, and initiating persons as Christian disciples.*

*These services are offered as models. Presiding ministers and worship planners are encouraged to adapt and use them as local custom and needs require. What is important is not the specific texts but faithful enactment of the gospel for the sake of Christ's disciple-making work in the lives of the people. Additions of music and movement that will amplify the congregation's hospitality and relationship to the persons being initiated are strongly recommended.*

*Throughout the services that follow the terms* pastor *or* presider *are used interchangeably to designate the person who leads the services. Whether the presider is a bishop, an ordained elder, or a local pastor, the term is suitable and focuses attention on the function of the person presiding.* Assisting minister *is used for any lay or ordained persons who are assisting the pastor/presider in leading worship. When the catechist is designated, it is because he or she has a particular role in relationship to persons being guided through the processes of Christian initiation. In some cases, the catechist may also be serving as an assisting minister.*

*Local churches may reproduce for worship and educational purposes any of the worship services in Part Two for a one-time use, provided the following copyright notice is included: Reprinted by permission from* Come to the Waters © *1996 Discipleship Resources.*

## Chapter One

# SERVICES FOR THE INTIATION OF ADULTS
## INTRODUCTION

Christian initiation is a process that shapes and celebrates conversion in the context of worship, Scripture, prayer, and ministry in daily life. The process consists of four stages and four services that bridge from one stage to the next. The stages and rites are designed to bring adults preparing for baptism into the life of faith and into full, conscious participation in the church's ministry of worship and witness. The word *adult* as used here includes youth who are seeking God and desire to know the way of Christ.

The initiation of adults focuses on conversion in the context of baptism as entrance into a covenantal relationship with the triune God and with the church. For this reason, it is critical that pastors and leaders, along with the whole congregation, understand that Christian initiation is much more substantive than a program that can be added to the current activities of congregational life. Christian initiation is more than a tool for church growth. Christian initiation is a long-term reorientation of the congregation's life to emphasize baptism and the missionary imperative of the gospel in an unbelieving world. It is God's call to recover the evangelical and sacramental balance that God gives to the church in baptism.

## RECOVERING THE STRUCTURES
## FOR MAKING AND SUSTAINING CHRISTIANS

Many, if not most, United Methodist congregations have lost a fundamental structure of their tradition: the systematic and continuous formation of disciples in "a company of [persons] having the *form* and seeking the *power* of godliness, united in order to pray together, to receive the word of exhortation, and to watch over one another in love, that they may help each other to work out their salvation."[63] This was not mere rhetoric in the Methodist movement in eighteenth century England. John Wesley and other methodical leaders formed into groups called classes those who responded to the revival. The classes were not a substitute for the church, which offered historic worship and the sacramental life. Rather, the groups ensured that those who had been given the form of godliness in baptism and in life in the church, had a structure in which to find and live in the power of godliness. The Methodist Societies and classes were little churches in the big church *(ecclesiolae in ecclesia)*.

Each class met weekly under the supervision of a reliable guide called a class leader. The class provided each person a setting for giving an account of how he or she had lived a rule of Christian life, called the General Rules. The General Rules were three simple and unconditional expectations that defined Christian living and offered guidance to disciples who hoped to live in the power of godliness. They were

1. to do no harm ("avoiding evil of every kind") so as not to sin against God and neighbor;
2. to do good so as to serve God and neighbor;
3. to use the means of grace (listed as the public worship of God, the ministry of the Word through reading and preaching, the Lord's Supper, family and private prayer, searching the Scriptures, and fasting or abstinence)[64]

Since all were expected to be in a class, continuous participation in a small group was also considered an essential means of grace. The General Rules can be found most readily in *The United Methodist Book of Discipline* (1992, ¶ 67). The first two (doing no evil and doing good) were each followed by a list of specifics. For example, "By doing no harm" was followed by "such as: The taking of the name of God in vain. The profaning the day of the Lord . . . Drunkenness . . . Slaveholding . . . Fighting . . .Uncharitable or unprofitable conversation . . .Doing what we know is not for the glory of God [which continues with more specifics]." "By doing good . . . to all" was followed by "To their bodies . . . [feeding, clothing, visiting, helping] . . . To their souls . . . "instructing, reproving, or exhorting" and "trampling under foot that enthusiastic doctrine that 'we are not to do good unless *our hearts be free to it.'*"[65] The impact of the General Rules was that no one could avoid the real world and the needs of others in the name of piety. Nor was anyone to live under love's imperative without grace sufficient for love's task.

Christian initiation calls for a similar formation (*catechesis*) to be replanted in congregational life both to form and to support living disciples and to create a context in which new disciples are made.

## CATECHESIS

Christian initiation is the congregation's work of teaching the Christian faith and life. The Greek word for this task and process is *catechesis*. The Methodist class meetings were a form of catechesis: In classes, which were primarily oral and relational, people were welcomed and formed in practical faith for daily life. Modern day catechesis encompasses all the forms, approaches, and methodologies used to guide seekers to the Christian faith and form disciples.

Catechesis should not be confused with memorization of answers to questions. That form of instruction focuses on information and a classroom model of education. The model proposed here is of the apprentice and the master. Ancient and contemporary catechesis, which this resource proposes, is one of experience followed by reflection. The approach is grounded in relationships of reliable guides and persons who are seeking to know the way of dying and rising with Christ in daily life (Romans 6:3-11; Galatians 2:20). In contrast to conversion of the intellect by chalkboard and chalk, this form of catechesis and conversion grows out of the "bed-side ministrations to the dying."[66] The catechetical journey aims at the conversion of a person's whole way of life, especially the affections of the heart and will, from which his or her words and deeds come forth.

## CONVERSION AND FORMATION
## ORDERED BY APPROACHING THRESHOLDS

The model for this pattern of catechesis comes to us from the ancient church. There, the community and its leaders walked with people who were being drawn by the Spirit into the church and its way of life. The ancient church knew that people seeking God in Christ had to take a series of steps. The distance was simply too great to be made in one step. The risks and changes called for in baptism were too great to be undertaken without examination and experience. For that reason, the church used images such as journey or gestation for the kind of process in which the catechumens participated.

As in the ways of the ancient church, the contemporary steps or thresholds for approaching baptism through initiation are not arbitrary or organizational. These thresholds of readiness are raised by the horizon of baptism itself. Candidates will be asked: Do you renounce the spiritual forces of wickedness and reject the evil powers of this world? Do you repent of your sin? Do you accept the freedom and power God gives you to resist evil, injustice, and oppression in whatever forms they present themselves? Do you confess Jesus Christ as your Savior? Do you put your whole trust in his grace and promise to serve him as your Lord? Do you promise to serve Jesus Christ in union with the church?[67]

People cannot come suddenly to questions like these, particularly those who have had little or no prior experience of faith and life with the church. Inquirers need guidance and time in which to experience prayer, to hear the Word of God, to participate in the ministry and worship of the church, to become aware of their need for deliverance, and to live with mentors of the faith.

The stages and rites of Christian initiation come before and after the sacrament of baptism. These stages and rites provide the essential preparation and integration needed by those being born into eternal life and the reign of God.

## THRESHOLDS OF READINESS

**1. Inquiry**

Persons discover and explore their experience of the nearness of the reign of God (Mark 1:15) in order to discern their response to the **threshold question: What do you seek?**

**Issue:** Quest for connection (How do your longings and your story connect with God's story?) Are you willing to reorder your life in order to hear and follow Jesus Christ?

**Process:** Evangelization—pre-conversion (pre-catechesis)

**Focus:** Telling life-stories, finding language to form questions, and answering the inquirer's questions

**Congregation's role:** hospitality, friendship, faith-sharing, discernment of questions

*Leads to welcome of inquirers.*
*Threshold question: What do you seek?*

## 2. Formation

The church accompanies persons seeking participation in the reign of God so that they may discern the answer to next **threshold questions: Do you desire to be baptized? Do you desire life with the church?**

**Issue**: Testing the depth and perseverance of one's desire to explore life as a Christian and to live as a disciple

**Process**: Hearing the Word and responding in worship, prayer, small group, ministry

**Focus**: Public participation in hearing and responding to the Word of God and discovery of self in relation to the gospel

**Congregation's role**: Coaching hearers in discipleship

*Leads to calling hearers to be candidates for baptism. Threshold questions: Do you desire to be baptized? Do you desire life with the church?*

## 3. Intensive Preparation

The church calls candidates to belong to the reign of God through baptism so that they may be prepared to answer the next **threshold questions: Do you renounce the spiritual forces of wickedness, and repent of your sin? Do you confess Jesus Christ as Savior and Lord?**

**Issue**: Saying *no* to sin and evil and finding the power and freedom to say *yes* to Christ

**Process**: Examination of the heart (self-searching and repentance) and enlightenment.

**Focus**: Encounter of the inner-self with Jesus and accepting Christ's call to belong to the reign of God

**Congregation's role**: Standing with the candidates in the light of Christ; being transparent about our own needs, struggles, and pilgrimage

*Leads to baptism as new birth, and participation in the death and resurrection of Christ. Threshold questions: Do you renounce the spiritual forces of wickedness, and repent of your sin? Do you confess Jesus Christ as Savior and Lord?*

**4. Integration**

The church rejoices with persons who now share in Christ's royal priesthood, and participate in being a living sacrament in daily life ministry. **Threshold questions: How will you endeavor to follow Jesus Christ under the guidance of the Holy Spirit? What is your sense of calling? What support do you need from other Christians in order to continue as Christ's faithful disciple?**

**Issues:** Discovery of one's self as part of a sacramental community, discernment of special calling and spiritual gifts, and clarity about ongoing participation in mutual support for the life of discipleship

**Process:** Continuation of discovery and discernment in worship, reflection on Scriptures, formational groups, prayer, and ministry

**Focus:** The church in worship, fellowship, and service as a living sacrament of Jesus Christ

**Congregation's role**: Getting to know the newly baptized, affirming them in ministry, and inviting them into ongoing mutual accountability for discipleship

*Leads to ongoing discipleship using the means of grace and living out of the baptismal covenant. Threshold questions: How will you endeavor to follow Jesus Christ under the guidance of the Holy Spirit? What is your sense of calling? What support do you need from other Christians in order to continue as Christ's faithful disciple?*

Christian initiation is an ordered formation (*catechesis*) in which the whole congregation participates. The converting community is itself converted in the process of walking with those Christ is making his disciples.

## COMMENTARY ON THE STAGES AND SERVICES

### STAGE ONE: INQUIRY

Persons drawn to the transforming reality of God's presence and action in their lives come from a wide range of backgrounds. Some come from non-Christian contexts. Others have had experience in the Christian community, though they were never baptized. Some have been deeply wounded in their past experience with the church. Some have significant background knowledge of the Christian faith, but have little experience of the disciplines of the Christian life. Others have no links to the

Christian faith and its story. In the inquiry stage, the congregation invites seekers just as they are to come with their questions and stories and to meet with others who are seeking God and God's power.

The focus is the seeker's search for belonging, love, and meaning. At this stage, many will not know or say that they are seeking faith. Their words and experiences will not fit neatly into theological or church language. They come from another world of experience; they come as they are with all of their rough edges and intensely personal experience with the surrounding culture.

Through hospitality, friendship, listening, and telling about faith in daily life, disciples in the congregation meet, know, and care for people on their quest. This evangelization may or may not happen in church buildings, scheduled worship, or social ministry. Believers befriend seeking persons and invite them to tell the story of their search for God; believers listen to their questions; tell the story of God's good news in Jesus; and care for them with love, respect, and expectation of the gracious action of the Holy Spirit.

During this period, believers supported by their leaders, help inquirers to discern the answer to the questions: What are you seeking? What is happening in your life that prompts your search? For many inquirers, their experience of the search will be personal, mysterious, raw, and inarticulate. Gentleness and sensitivity on the part of Christians who relate to them are essential. In this stage, the needs and the pace of the inquirer must be given priority.

In time, and in order to assist the inquirers in gaining clarity about their quest, sponsors and leaders may encourage them to struggle with questions like these: What place does faith have in your life? Are you ready to reorder your life in order to hear and follow the call of Jesus Christ? Are you willing to do this by making a disciplined exploration of Christian living and service to God and neighbor?

Sponsors should be assigned as early in this stage as the seeking person seems to welcome the support and attention of another person during his or her quest. The sponsor may be the person who has already befriended the seeker in a setting outside the congregation. If seekers come to worship on their own, church leaders will need to choose and assign appropriate sponsors.

In some settings, small groups will be formed for weekly conversation. In others, the initial stage may be carried out between the sponsor and inquirer. The critical dimension is that the first stage be the beginning of an accompanied journey and a time when the seeker comes to terms with his or her search for belonging, meaning, and love in relationship to God in Christ.

## SERVICE ONE: WELCOMING HEARERS

The first stage concludes when there is discernment by inquirers, sponsors, and the catechist that the inquirer desires to enter into the reign of God and to publicly participate in the life of the church. While the Christian faith is personal, it is not a private or self-designed relationship to God. When a person demonstrates a hunger to share publicly in the communal journey of God's people and to know Jesus Christ, he or she has approached the threshold of the next stage. "A Service for Welcoming

Hearers" (p. 109) allows the inquirer to openly confess this desire and asks the congregation to welcome and celebrate God's grace working in the inquirer's life.

The service of welcome may be held at any time of the year. Since it is a public act it should take place during a Sunday service of worship so that the congregation is present. If a person is uncomfortable with such a public welcome, he or she probably needs more time.

"A Service for Welcoming Hearers" includes questions concerning the intent of the inquirer, the congregation's welcome, questions concerning the congregation's intention to support and care for the one seeking to learn the way of love and life, an invitation to the inquirer to join the congregation in its regular hearing of the Word of God, the ritual of marking the newly welcomed with the sign of the cross, and the congregation's offering its prayers for the new hearer. The inquirer now becomes a hearer.

## STAGE TWO: FORMATION

This stage is marked by the association of the hearer with the congregation in its public worship, prayer, study of the story of salvation, and ministry in daily life. The stage focuses on disciplined exploration of Christian living and on learning to live out the great commandments to love God and neighbor. Throughout the stage, sponsors and the catechist meet regularly with the hearers to pray and reflect on the lectionary passages or other appropriate Scripture texts used in Sunday worship. The needs of each hearer determine the length and flow of the process in this stage. The congregation supports the hearers with prayer, both public and private, and the attentive company of sponsors.

The hearers are encouraged to grow in attentiveness to the voice of God as they learn of the way of discipleship and Christian faith. While the focus of this stage is primarily formational, necessary information about Christian tradition and practice should be made available to the hearers. Sponsors observe and support the hearers' unfolding conversion and discipleship. The catechist guides the overall process of formation in faith by creating settings in which the hearers can experience the grace and power of God.

In formational groups or with their sponsors, hearers experience a pattern of accountability in which they are supported by others. In practicing the basics of worship, devotion, justice, and compassion in daily life, they experience the Christian life lived in community.[68] Members of the congregation may be called upon to help hearers learn the basics of Christian living and to witness by inviting hearers to go with them to their places of ministry and work. Significant time should be spent in service to the poor, through the ongoing ministries of the congregation. The pastor and congregation need to be sure that social ministry to the neglected and oppressed is integral to congregational life and formation. Reflecting on the experience of ministry allows each hearer to discern the voice of God in daily life and to be formed by Jesus' call to witness by serving neighbors (Luke 10:25-37).

The connection between what the risen Lord is doing and what is needed in the various settings of daily life is a primary focus in this and all of the stages of Christian initiation. Weekly reflection in formational groups should consider the connections between faith and life, asking how God is active in these areas: family, leisure, work, community, church and national or global concerns.

When the congregation invites hearers to reflect on and discuss questions about faith and life, it encourages them find ways to talk about their story, to discern the guidance of the Holy Spirit, and to affirm their ministry in daily life.

Each congregation will need to choose the most suitable time for the formational group to meet. Some may choose to send hearers and their sponsors to meet after the reading of the Scriptures and the sermon, while the congregation continues to worship. Other congregations may find that a time other than Sunday morning works better. The ancient church dismissed the hearers (catechumens) from worship so that they would not be present for the Eucharist until they had received baptism. (See Appendix 2.)

During this period, as well as in the inquiry stage, sponsors, the catechist, and the pastor should be alert to readiness in the hearers to respond to the justifying grace of God. Hearers, growing in their sense of need for the grace of forgiveness, healing, and acceptance by God, will welcome the invitation to put their trust in Christ and his redeeming love. This evangelical work by leaders is essential to guiding hearers to a balanced experience of grace and works, redemption and obedience.

The threshold to which all this experience and reflection leads is a growing desire to belong to and live with the gospel community. When the hearer knows that he or she desires to be baptized and live within the church, and when this is out-wardly manifest in the hearer's life, the sponsor and the catechist can witness to the hearer's readiness to become a candidate for baptism. This calling and witness takes place in "A Service for Calling Persons to Baptism."

## SERVICE TWO: CALLING PERSONS TO BAPTISM

During worship on the First Sunday in Lent[69], those hearers who are convinced that they desire to live their lives within the baptismal covenant are presented and called by the church to baptism. In this service (pp. 113-115), the hearers are questioned concerning their intention to be baptized, and the day of their baptism is announced. Sponsors witness to the conversion process that has been taking place in each hearer. The congregation reaffirms its support and offers its prayers for the hearer, who now becomes a candidate for baptism.

## STAGE THREE: INTENSIVE PREPARATION

This stage takes place during the days leading up to the announced date of baptism. The focus of reflection during this stage anticipates the questions candidates will be asked at baptism concerning their renunciation of evil and sin and their profession of faith in Christ as Savior and Lord. During the intensive preparation stage, leaders and sponsors encourage candidates to recognize and resist evil and injustice, and to become participants in the reign of God in the world. Questions like "What must change (die) in you in order that Christ's reign of love and justice may flourish in your life?" and "How will you live for Jesus in your daily life?" will help the candidates examine themselves in preparation for initiation. Questions of the heart are particularly pertinent: What desires and affections need realignment for you to follow Christ with your whole heart?

This stage includes a series of worship acts that signal intensive preparation for Christian initiation, including the handing on or giving of the Apostles' Creed, on the third Sunday in Lent, (p. 116) and the Lord's Prayer, on the fifth Sunday in Lent (p. 117). Sponsors and catechist continue to meet regularly with the candidates for prayer and reflection on worship, Scripture, and ministry.

Preparation for the depth of the questions to be asked at baptism is essential. The ancient church used forms of exorcism called scrutinies as preparation for baptism. Contemporary Christian initiation processes are less a direct confrontation with evil and more a time of prayer for the candidates as they stand in the light of Christ. Worship and formational group sessions during this stage may include time for the examination of conscience, particularly on the third, fourth, and fifth Sundays in Lent. The purpose is not to evoke guilt or to despair about character flaws. The examination of conscience is a means of grace. Communal self-searching and repentance, guided by trust in the Holy Spirit, uncovers what is weak, tempting, defective, blind, or sinful in the heart and strengthens what is strong, good, and increasingly given to Christ as Savior and Lord.

During Holy Week or another period before baptism, the congregation may design special opportunities for prayer and reflection on Jesus' passion and death. Such experiences could include a retreat, a vigil at the church, or some other experience that engages the candidates and offers them the congregation's prayerful attention and support. The ancient disciplines of fasting, examination of the conscience, and prayer may be employed in appropriate ways to assist the candidates to be emotionally and spiritually ready for baptism.

## SERVICE THREE: HOLY BAPTISM

On the announced day of the celebration of the baptismal covenant (preferably at the Easter Vigil or on Easter Day), the candidates are baptized into the Lord's passion, death, and resurrection. Full Christian initiation, as reflected in "Services Of The Baptismal Covenant" (*UMH*, 33 and *UMBOW*, 81), includes water baptism, the laying on of hands, and the Eucharist. Adequate planning for an undiminished celebration of Easter and the entrance of the newly baptized into eternal life is strongly encouraged.

## STAGE FOUR: INTEGRATION INTO THE COMMUNITY AND CALL TO MISSION AND LIFE IN THE SACRAMENTS

During the Great Fifty Days, the newly baptized explore the sacraments of Baptism and Holy Communion as God's continuing grace and God's call to ministry and witness in daily life. Sponsors, the catechist, and the pastor support them in focusing on questions such as these:

- As a baptized, table-sharing Christian, how will you endeavor to follow Jesus Christ under the guidance of the Holy Spirit?

- What is your sense of calling? How will your life be offered as a living sacrifice in the community of Christ's royal priesthood and in the world? How is God calling you to ministry in daily life? Who or what in your world needs the love of God and your active attention?

- What support will you need from other Christians in order to continue as Christ's faithful disciple? How has being in the formation group shaped your life? How is Christ calling you to participate in mutual support for faithful discipleship?

As with the previous stages, the lectionary readings provide the primary focus for weekly worship and for ongoing discussion and reflection in formation groups during the integration stage.

Since the newly baptized have been incorporated into the community of the faithful, Sunday worship during the Great Fifty Days should emphasize their interaction with the faithful. Joyful celebration and settings for informal welcome and fellowship should be planned.

## SERVICE FOUR: AFFIRMATION OF MINISTRY

On the Day of Pentecost, the newly baptized come forward and stand before or among the congregation. Individuals may tell about specific forms of service or witness they have begun or to which they feel called. The congregation offers prayer for them and celebrates the ministry of others who are reaffirming their discipleship and affirming particular callings. (See p. 120.)

Settings and opportunities for ongoing support of discipleship and ministry in daily life are essential to fruitful and faithful congregational life. Small groups, in which persons can continue to reflect on the Scriptures and daily experience and watch over one another in love, are essential for sustained participation in the ministry of the people of God. Entrance into the baptismal covenant must never be seen as arrival or graduation. Congregational leaders and sponsors should encourage new Christians to participate in ongoing small groups where they can grow and find mutual support for living out the cost and the joy of discipleship.

## A Service for Welcoming Hearers

*This service is designed to be used within a full service of worship. The service is for use with persons who have inquired about the gospel, spent time with sponsors, told their stories, tested their motives, and are ready to take a first public step declaring their desire to seek life in Christ.*

*The sponsors and the inquirers gather outside the church or in the entry area. When the pastor has given an introduction about what is to take place, the congregation may sing an appropriate song, psalm, or hymn as it turns toward the place of welcome. The presiding and assisting ministers, including the catechist, move to the place where the inquirers are assembled with their sponsors.*

*The service of welcome invites adaptation, especially at the Greeting [1] and Opening Dialogue [3]. In adapting the service, leaders should maintain brevity and focus while seeking to embody the hospitality and welcome of the gospel.*

*This service may also be used following the sermon. In such cases, "Invitation to Come and Hear the Word of God," [7] should be omitted and the person to be welcomed should come before the congregation from his or her seat.*

*For simplicity, the text of the service is oriented to the welcome of one inquirer. More than one inquirer may be welcomed in the same service by making minor adjustments in language.*

+

### Welcoming a Hearer

1. **Greeting**

   *The pastor stands before the inquirer and greets him or her in a warm and hospitable way. Addressing the inquirer, the sponsor, and the congregation, the pastor expresses the joy and delight of the church in welcoming persons who have been drawn to the story of Jesus and the life of faith. The catechist may welcome the inquirer with words and gestures that invite him or her to stand before the people. All may join in singing an appropriate hymn, song, or psalm.*

2. **Presentation**

   *The sponsor, standing with the inquirer, says:*

   I present _____(*name*), who desires to learn the way of Christ.

3. **Opening Dialogue**

   *When the inquirer has been presented, the presider asks:*

   _____ (*name*), what do you seek?

   *The inquirer answers with one of the statements that follow or with another appropriate response.*

   **I seek life in Jesus Christ**
   or
   **I seek to know Jesus Christ**

*When the inquirer has been appropriately prepared, the pastor has the option of asking other questions about his or her intentions. Particular stories or experiences that have brought the inquirer to this step on the journey of faith may be told.*

### 4. First Acceptance of the Gospel

*The catechist or another congregational leader addresses the inquirer:*
Jesus said, "I am the light of the world. Whoever follows me
will never walk in darkness but will have the light of life."
You have been drawn to Christ's light,
and the way of the gospel is open before you.
Journey with us and learn to trust Christ.
Grow to believe in him with all your heart.
Jesus will show you how to love God and to love your neighbor.
This love is his command, and he will lead you.
Are you ready, with the help of God, to live this life with us?
**I am.**
Will you be faithful in attending the worship of God and in receiving direction as a disciple?
**I will.**
Will you listen to the Word of God and open your heart and mind to welcome Jesus as your Lord and Savior?
**I will, with God's help.**

### 5. Commitment of Sponsor and Congregation

*The catechist says to the sponsor and to the entire congregation:*
Will you care for _____ (name)
with your prayer and companionship?
**With gladness, I will.**
Will you help _____ (name) by word and example to know
God and to discover the way of following Jesus Christ?
**I will.**

*The sponsor lays hands on the shoulders of the candidate while the pastor or other leader addresses all who are gathered:*
The Lord be with you.
**And also with you.**
Let us pray.
Almighty God, like a shepherd searching for lost sheep
and like a parent waiting to welcome home a wandering child,
you have called _____ (name) to know your way and love.
Now _____ (name) has turned to seek you.
Today, _____ (name) has declared *his/her* desire to know the way of love
and life in Jesus Christ.
Today, we welcome _____ (name) as a hearer in the way of eternal life.

We bless you and praise you for what you are doing in _____ *(name)*
and among us.

*All may sing a song of welcome or praise.*
  *(Suggestions from UMH: 789, response only or 769, response only*
  *Suggestions from UMBOW: 198, 200)*

## 6. Marking with the Sign of the Cross
*The sponsor traces the cross on the hearer's forehead, as the presiding minister says:*
  Receive the mark of the cross on your forehead,
  as a sign of the way you are to walk,
  and as a sign of Christ with you in strength and love.
  May the power of the Holy Spirit enable you to know and to follow our
  Lord, Jesus Christ.
    **Amen.**

*The people may respond saying or singing:*
  **Glory and praise to you, Almighty God.**

## 6A. Optional Marking with the Sign of the Cross
*The presiding minister may continue, as a sponsor traces a cross on each part of*
*the candidate's body as it is mentioned.[70]*
  Receive the cross on your ears, that you may hear the gospel of Christ,
  the Word of life.
    **Glory and praise to you, Almighty God.**
  Receive the cross on your eyes, that you may see the light of Christ,
  illumination for your way.
    **Glory and praise to you, Almighty God.**
  Receive the cross on your lips, that you may sing the praise of Christ,
  the joy of the church.
    **Glory and praise to you, Almighty God.**
  Receive the cross on your heart, that God may dwell there by faith.
    **Glory and praise to you, Almighty God.**
  Receive the cross on your shoulders, that you may bear the gentle yoke of Christ.
    **Glory and praise to you, Almighty God.**
  Receive the cross on your hands, that God's mercy may be known in your work.
    **Glory and praise to you, Almighty God.**
  Receive the cross on your feet, that you may walk in the way of Christ.
    **Glory and praise to you, Almighty God.**

*All may sing an appropriate acclamation or hymn.*
  *Suggestion from UMBOW: "Amen, Praise the Father" (178)*
  *Suggestion from UMH: "Pues Si Vivimos (When We Are Living") refrain only (356)*

7. **Invitation to Come and Hear the Word of God**

   *A representative of the church invites the hearer to listen to the Word of God using these or similar words:*

   > God's word is like bread for our hearts; we cannot live without it.
   > God's word is like rain that comes down upon the earth, bringing forth fruit in our lives.
   > Come and be with us as a hearer of the Word of God.
   > Let the Word of God guide your way and bring you to everlasting life.

   *Here the sponsor may present a Bible to the hearer, as the catechist says:*

   > Receive the good news of Jesus Christ, the Son of God.
   > Read and listen for the voice of Jesus, the living Lord.
   > Listen to hear, trust, and follow him.

   *The hearer and the sponsor take their seats. The worship continues with the reading of the Scriptures and the sermon. When this service is used following the sermon, the worship continues with the Concerns and Prayers, including prayers for the hearer.*

   *Note: If the candidate desires to renounce a former way of worship, the pastor may use an appropriately worded renunciation after the first question of the Opening Dialogue [3]. When persons have been adherents of a religion or religious system incompatible with the Christian faith and there is discernment that this is a stumbling block for the inquirer and troubling to his or her conscience, the pastor may counsel with the person to resolve his or her conflicted sense of loyalty. The option of renouncing a former way of worship and faith anticipates renunciation of all that is contrary to Christ in the service of the baptismal covenant (see UMH, p. 34, section 4)*

## A Service for Calling Persons to Baptism

*This service is normally used on the First Sunday in Lent. When persons are being prepared for baptism in the Advent-Christmas cycle, it is used on the First Sunday of Advent.*

*The service presupposes that those who are to be called to baptism have undergone conversion in belief and action and have been formed in the Christian way of love and faith. Appropriate face-to-face conferences and discernment of readiness by those who have worked with the candidates must precede the service so that any hint of mere formality is avoided.*

*The sermon should be appropriate to the actual situation and should address both the congregation and the hearers, calling them to journey in prayer and discipline toward the waters of baptism.*

*The service follows the sermon. During a hymn of response, the hearers, their sponsors, and the catechist come forward and stand before the assembly and the pastor. If space allows, the congregation may gather around the hearers and their sponsors. (When both adults and children are being called to baptism in the same service, the service for calling to baptism on page 133 should be used.)*

For simplicity, the text of the service is oriented to calling more than one person to baptism. Changes can easily be made to address one person.

## +
## Calling Persons to Baptism

### 1. Presentation
*The hearers who are to be presented face the people. The catechist addresses the pastor and the congregation.*

Dear friends in Christ, *these persons* who stand before you today have been listening to the Word of God with us.

_____ (*names of hearers*) have been learning our way of life in Jesus Christ.

We have given *them* our support with friendship, prayer, and example.
God's transforming grace has been at work among us and in *them*.
As *Easter* draws near, *they* ask to participate in the sacraments.
Let us hear of their journey and of God's call to Holy Baptism.

*(When the date of baptism will be at a service other than the Easter Vigil or Easter, the leader may substitute the appropriate words, such as " As the Baptism of the Lord draws near, . . .")*

### 2. Affirmation by Sponsors
*The pastor, speaking to the sponsors, says:*
Dear brothers and sisters, as sponsors and friends of ____ (*names of hearers*),

you know that *they* seek initiation into Christ's holy church.
We want to know that *they* are prepared to enter life in Christ.
You have walked with *them* on a journey of conversion.
You have prayed for *them* to know and to heed the voice of Christ.
You have witnessed *their* love of God and of neighbor in daily living.
As God is your witness, tell us of *their* readiness
to obey Christ's call to life in the baptismal covenant.

*Have they* faithfully joined in the worship of God?
   **They have.**
*Have they* heard God's word and followed Jesus in their daily life?
   **They have.**
*Have they* come to know Christ's story and way, and *have they* engaged in
ministry with the poor and the neglected?
   **They have.**

*Here each sponsor may speak in a brief and focused way of the hearers' growth
and courage in learning the Christian life. The affirmation should be expressed in
words that witness to God's gracious work in the hearers' hearts, minds, and
actions. Each sponsor's witness should express God's love and should neither
praise the hearers nor expose or embarrass them.*

*When each sponsor has made his or her witness, the pastor addresses the con-
gregation saying:*
   Brothers and sisters, you have heard the witness of *these persons* concerning
   the hearers. Will you support (*names of hearers*) and continue to welcome
   them with your prayers and loving actions, as we journey toward *Easter* and
   the waters of baptism?
      **With glad and expectant hearts, we will!**

3. **Invitation and Call**
   *The presider says to the hearers:*
      You have heard the affirmation of your *sponsors*
      and the promise of love from the people of God.
      You have heard the call of Jesus and we ask you to answer clearly:
      Do you desire to be baptized at *Easter*?
         **Yes, that is my desire.**

4. **Declaration and Charge**
   *The presider, calling each hearer by name, says:*
      _____, (*name*) in the name of Jesus Christ, we call you to life in the
      Church and to initiation into the mystery of Jesus' death and resurrection
      through baptism at the *Easter Vigil*.
   *Each candidate responds:*
      **Thanks be to God!**

*When each candidate has been called, the presider assures the candidates of God's faithfulness and encourages them with these or similar words:*
> You are learning to trust God with your life.
> God is faithful and will complete the work that God has begun in you.
> Now you are called to enter, with courage and faith, into a *forty day* retreat.
> Stand in the light, and Christ will illumine and strengthen your hearts.
> Resist evil and rely on Jesus' grace for endurance.
> With us, follow Jesus into the truth and life of the gospel
> *at the festival of his death and resurrection*
> [or, *at the festival of his baptism,* or other appropriate words].

*Then the presider turns to the sponsors and charges them saying:*
> You have spoken with favor concerning *the candidates* for baptism.
> Receive *them* as chosen in the Lord and
> support *them* in keeping the disciplines of prayer, fasting,
> meditation on the Word of God, and examination of conscience.
> Share with *them* the risk of full conversion.

## 5. Concerns and Prayers
*The newly-called candidates and sponsors remain together before the congregation so that they may be included in the congregation's Concerns and Prayers. If the candidates are to leave for reflection on Scripture in a formational group, "Prayer Over the Candidates" [6] may take place and "Concerns and Prayers" [5] may follow the departure of the candidates and their sponsors.*

## 6. Prayer over the Candidates
*Each sponsor places a hand on the shoulder of the candidates; the presider extends hands over them, praying:*
> The Lord be with you.
> > **And also with you.**
> Let us pray:
> God of love and power,
> your purpose is to bring all creation within your saving embrace.
> Draw into Christ's life *these people,* whom you have chosen.
> By the power of your Spirit, bring *them to be true sons and daughters*
> of the gospel and adopt *them* by the mystery of your grace
> through Christ, our Lord.
> > **Amen.**

*Here the candidates and their sponsors return to their seats or go to a place for the meeting of their formational group. If they leave the service, they should be sent forth with a blessing and a call to hear the Word of God. The service continues to its conclusion.*

## PRAYERS AND RITES DURING INTENSIVE PREPARATION

*Conversion of heart, mind, and will to Jesus Christ is the work of the Holy Spirit. Christian initiation is the ordering of conversion by stages and by rites that serve as celebrations of the work of the Spirit in those being formed as Christian disciples. The congregation can prepare the way for continuing conversion by opening doors to new thresholds of faith and life.*

*The period of intensive preparation for baptism focuses intently on the gift of grace that God gives in baptism. Part of God's gift is incorporation into the faith and prayer of the church.*

*Use of these rites during worship on the Lord's Day strongly portrays the congregation's giving to the candidates the faith and prayer of the people of God.*

*The presiding minister and catechist may lead the congregation in these actions.*

✝

## HANDING ON THE FAITH OF THE CHURCH

*The congregation presents the candidates with a symbol of the faith of the church, the Apostles' Creed. The Apostles' Creed summarizes the central articles of our faith in the triune God. It connects Christians with their ecumenical heritage and links them to the apostolic faith and witness of the early church. As a baptismal creed, it serves as the basis for entrance into the baptismal covenant and helps the candidates to relate diverse scriptural texts to the essential narrative of God's saving action.*

*The act of presentation may take place following the sermon on the Third Sunday in Lent (or Advent) or another appropriate Sunday The examination of conscience follows this action.*

*The presider or the catechist calls the candidates and their sponsors to come forward and to stand before the people. The people may be invited to gather around them. Addressing the candidates, the presider says:*

Dear friends, you have been called to baptism
and to profess the faith of the church
with the words you speak and the lives you live.
Listen as we declare this confession of the faith
by which Christians are held together
in covenant with the Triune God.

*The candidates listen as the congregation hands on to them the faith of the church by reciting the Apostles' Creed. The presider may invite the congregation to extend hands toward the candidates during the recitation. When the recitation is concluded, prayer for the candidates may be offered using "Prayer Over Candidates" [6] in "A Service Calling Persons To Baptism." (See p. 115.)*

*The catechist may give each candidate a copy of the Apostles' Creed to memorize and to reflect upon in formational groups during the remaining weeks of Lent, Advent and Christmas or another suitable time period.*

*The service continues with the Concerns and Prayers.*

# ✛
# HANDING ON THE PRAYER OF THE CHURCH

*The congregation presents the candidates with the prayer Jesus gave to the disciples when he taught them to pray. The Lord's Prayer shapes the prayers of all who share Jesus' desire to know and do the will of God and is at the heart of the church's daily prayer.*

*The act of presentation may take place just prior to the Concerns and Prayers and following the examination of conscience on the Fifth Sunday in Lent (or the Sunday after Christmas or another suitable Sunday).*

*The presider or catechist calls the candidates to stand before the people. Addressing the candidates, the presider says:*

Dear friends,
hear the teaching the Lord Jesus gives
to those who seek to know and do the will of God.

*An assisting minister or a member of the congregation reads Matthew 6:7-13. In the reading, he or she may insert the text of the Lord's Prayer commonly prayed by the people. Even though the candidates may already know the Lord's Prayer, they should be instructed prior to the service to listen as the community hands on to them the prayer of the church.*

*Then the presider may invite the sponsors and the people to gather around the candidates. Inviting the candidates to kneel, the presider addresses them in these or similar words:*

In the name of the Lord who has called you to life among us,
we hand on to you our common prayer
and we call you to share our life of prayer
for the people of God and for the world.
Take your place among us as people who pray.

*Here all may extend hands over the candidates as they say or sing the Lord's Prayer.*

*Prayer for the candidates may be offered immediately after the Lord's Prayer, or during the Concerns and Prayers that follow, using "Prayer over the Candidates" [6] in "A Service for Calling Persons to Baptism," (p. 115).*

*Each candidate may be given a copy of the Lord's Prayer before returning to his or her place.*

# ✛
# EXAMINATION OF CONSCIENCE

*Candidates are now at the threshold of baptism and entrance into the reign of God as committed disciples of the crucified and risen Lord. Jesus, who calls them to baptism and faithful discipleship, stands before them as liberator and deliverer from evil, sin, and death. Examinations of conscience are times of prayer with the congre-*

gation that move beyond understanding ideas to yielding habits, attitudes, percep-tions, loyalties, and one's hidden depths to Jesus as Savior and Lord. The congrega-tion's faith in the living Lord is the setting for this deeper work of the Spirit in conver-sion and transformation.

Examinations of conscience are times of grace and prayer. They are never to be occasions for probing or manipulation. The Spirit can and must be trusted to do the work of conversion. As prayer, examinations of conscience are settings in which the candidates are supported in their encounter with Jesus, who invites all to drink from the well of salvation, opens blind eyes, and raises the dead to life. In this encounter, the congregation prays on candidates' behalf for the grace to say no to sin and evil in order to be free to say yes to Jesus Christ in daily life.

Examinations of conscience may take place as responses to the proclamation on the third, fourth, and fifth Sundays in Lent (or on the third and fourth Sundays of Advent and the first Sunday after Christmas).

When the candidates are called forward, the sponsors should stand or kneel beside them and place their hands on the candidates' shoulder. As in "Handing on the Faith of the Church" and "Handing on the Prayer of the Church," the presider may invite the people to gather around the candidates for this time of prayer.

One of the following or similar prayers may be used. The prayers should be adapted in ways that include the imagery of the lessons for the day, particularly the gospel reading.

The people may be invited to respond to each petition by saying or singing, **Lord, hear our prayer.**

A.  The Lord be with you.
    **And also with you.**
    Let us pray to the Lord, who knows _____ (*names of candidates*) better than *they* know *themselves*. (pause)
    Let us pray that Jesus will illumine the darkness and bring to light in *them* all that is not free to serve God.
        *silent prayer followed by response*
    Let us pray for the Lord to deliver *them* from the power of sin and temptation that enslaves and twists *their* desire to love and follow the Lord, Jesus Christ.
        *silent prayer followed by response*
    Let us ask the Lord to search *their* hearts and wills, and to purify *their* conscience of all that is not ready to be joined to Christ in loving God and neighbor.
        *silent prayer followed by response*
    Let us thank the Lord for *them* and for God's grace that brings full repentance and freedom to spirits, minds, and bodies.
        *silent prayer followed by response*

    *The pastor and the congregation may extend hands over the candidates as the presider prays:*
        Lord Jesus, you alone can cleanse and free us for joyful obedience.

We thank you for hearing our prayer for _____ (*names of candidates*).
We thank you that you are bringing *them* from sin to righteousness, from blindness to sight, from death to life. By your Holy Spirit, keep them forever as your own. Fill them with love and faith and hope.
**Amen.**

*Here an appropriate song, hymn, or psalm may be sung.*

B.  The Lord be with you.
    **And also with you.**
    Let us pray to the Lord for _____ (*names of candidates*) whom, God has called to baptism.
    Lord Jesus, you know our thirsts; remove from the candidates all of the longings that draw *them* away from you.
        *silent prayer followed by response*
    Lord Jesus, you know our blindness; open *their* hearts and minds to see and to yield to you anything that stands in the way of *their* saying *yes* to you.
        *silent prayer followed by response*
    Lord Jesus, you are the resurrection and the life; call _____ (*names of candidates*) out of the grave of old hurts so that *they* may enjoy eternal life with you and all your people.
        *silent prayer followed by response*

*The pastor and the congregation may extend hands over the candidates as the presider prays:*
Lord Jesus, you made no truce with evil, and you stood the test of temptation by holding to the Word of God; help and deliver *these people whom* you have called to baptism.
Drive from *them* all doubt and resistance.
Set *them* free from the shackles of old patterns and addictions.
Lift *them* from the grip of death.
Cancel the power of sin and fear.
Awaken in *them* a true sense of your majesty and authority.
We ask this by the power of the Holy Spirit you have breathed upon us.
    **Amen.**

*An appropriate song, hymn, or psalm may be sung.*

*Suggested from UMH: See hymns on healing, numbers 262-266, and on repentance, numbers 349-358. Consider* "Jaya Ho (Victory Hymn)" (478); "Jesus, Lover of My Soul" (479); "Let My People Seek Their Freedom" (586); "It's Me, It's Me, O Lord" (352); "Spirit Song" (547). *Also see listings under* "Choruses" *on page 936.*

# ✛
## HOLY BAPTISM: THE BAPTISMAL COVENANT
### (at Easter Vigil, Easter Day, The Baptism of the Lord, or another appropriate day)

*Since the services of the Baptismal Covenant are readily available in the hymnal and the Book of Worship, they are not printed here. "The Baptismal Covenant I," pp. 33-39 in* The United Methodist Hymnal *and pp. 86-94 in* The United Methodist Book of Worship, *is the appropriate service to use for adult baptism. "The Baptismal Covenant III" is an alternative service.*

*When baptism occurs at the Easter Vigil, the resources of* The United Methodist Book of Worship, *369-376, should be used.*

*When baptism occurs on the Baptism of the Lord, baptism should be in the context of the service of Word and Table. The Book of Worship, 299-301, provides specific resources for the Baptism of the Lord.*

*Generous use of water, anointing with oil, and high celebration of the Eucharist, are recommended. Strong sacramental action will serve in building strong faith and a memorable initiation into Christ and the church.*

# ✛
## A SERVICE FOR AFFIRMATION OF MINISTRY IN DAILY LIFE

*In this service, the congregation recognizes and celebrates the witness and ministry of the newly baptized in the context of the whole congregation's ministry. While special focus is given to the commitment of the newly baptized, returning members, or members who are reaffirming their baptismal covenant, the service properly recognizes all who are in ministry in daily life.*

*If persons are baptized at Easter, this service is suitably incorporated into worship on the Day of Pentecost. If persons are baptized on the Baptism of the Lord, this service is appropriately included in worship on Transfiguration Sunday. If baptism occurred at some other time during the year, this service can be included in worship on some day that focuses on the work of the Holy Spirit or the witness of the church.*

*After the sermon, the pastor, a deacon, or another congregational leader invites all (including the newly baptized) who desire affirmation of ministry to come forward to stand before or among the congregation.*

*"An Order for Commitment to Christian Service," pp. 591-592, in* The United Methodist Book of Worship, *may be used as the structure for recognition and affirmation of service to Christ. This service aims at affirming ministry both in general terms and in connection with a specific vision of service in the world or in the church.*

*As an alternative introductory statement to the one in "An Order for Commitment to Christian Service," the leader may say:*

Brothers and sisters in Christ, on this *Day of Pentecost (Day of Transfiguration, or special day)*
we rejoice in the ministry of _____ *(names)*
and celebrate *their* love and work in service to Jesus Christ, our Lord.

*As suggested by the rubrics in the service on p. 591 in* UMBOW, *the pastor, a deacon, or another congregational leader may "briefly describe the form of service to which each person is being consecrated." In addition, some persons may wish to express in their own words or actions their sense of calling and vision for ministry.*

*The pastor, a deacon, or another congregational leader may ask each person:*
Having committed yourself to live out your baptismal covenant in daily witness and service, how will you endeavor to follow Jesus Christ under the guidance of the Holy Spirit?

*The service then continues with an act of consecration such as item 12 in "The Baptismal Covenant" (UMH, p. 37) or the prayer in "An Order for Commitment to Christian Service" (UMBOW, 591). Sponsors and other members of the congregation may join the pastor in laying hands on each person.*
*Careful planning of the service will prevent this time from being unduly hurried or lengthy. The sermon for this day should be brief and appropriate to the affirmation of the ministry the people of God.*

Chapter Two

# Services for the Intiation of Children
## Introduction

The pattern of Christian initiation for children is parallel to the pattern used with adults preparing for baptism. See "Adaptation of the Initiation Process—An Outline" on page 43 for ready comparison. There are four stages, each concluding with a service of celebration and transition to the next stage.

The process has a two-fold aim:

1.  Welcoming children for baptism;

2.  Welcoming and forming the parents as the primary sponsors for their children who are candidates for baptism.

Parents are not considered candidates except when they are also preparing for baptism. When parents are candidates for baptism or are preparing to reaffirm their baptismal vows, they appropriately participate in the process used for adults. Parents who are baptized should not be included in rites that are used with persons who are not baptized. Those who lead in the processes of Christian initiation will insure that they have opportunity to reflect on their ministry as parents.

The initiation of children requires that parents participate in a process of formation (catechesis) in preparing to celebrate the baptism of their children and the reaffirmation of their baptismal covenant. Children may be accepted for baptism through their parents' profession of faith. The stages of inquiry, formation, and intensive preparation pertain primarily to the parents when the child is an infant or young child. Subsequent to baptism, as children mature and their capacity for the life of faith and participation in the life of the congregation grows, they will participate in the processes of inquiry, formation, and intensive preparation.

## COMMENTARY ON THE STAGES AND SERVICES

### STAGE ONE:
### PARENTAL INQUIRY CONCERNING THE BAPTISM OF CHILDREN

This stage may begin as soon as parents begin adoption procedures or discover pregnancy. Sponsors and godparents are chosen in consultation with the pastor or catechist. Sponsors must be baptized persons and should be members of the congregation. Godparents need not be members of the congregation, but should be professing Christians.

Remembering that Christian initiation seeks to make the life of faith accessible to all, especially to those who are least familiar with the gospel and its call to life in Christ, leaders need to be flexible and sensitive with each family. While some prospective parents may be well-known and faithful participants in the congregation, others may not be as active in the church's life and may inquire about baptism late in their pregnancy or adoption process. The ministry of hospitality and listening will enable leaders to know how to meet inquirers where they are in their hopes and searching. Sponsors can take a special role in entering into the family's excitement.

Special care and clear instruction may be needed by many parents who inquire about baptism because the perception that baptism is a service provided by the church is still prevalent. This inheritance from Christendom rests on the notion that the services of the church can be paid for, as is sometimes the cases for weddings and funerals. Rather than a service for hire, pastors and congregation can offer a welcome and an invitation to discovery of life in the faith community.

At any point during this stage, the pastor and congregation may offer prayers celebrating pregnancy or preparation for adoption. This may be done in the home or during a regular service of worship. When done in a regular service, the blessing of expectant parents allows the congregation to see, meet, and pray for the family.

During the time of expectancy, parents, other children, godparents, and sponsors meet regularly with a catechist and other appropriate leaders for preparation as spiritual guides for the child they are about to welcome. The experiences of pregnancy or the adoption process, along with participation in worship, form the basis of reflection for the participants. It is particularly appropriate to reflect upon living out the baptismal covenant in marriage, family, and child-bearing as a vocation and as a primary opportunity for ministry in daily life.

In cases where the parents have not been baptized or formed in discipleship, they should be invited to participate in the inquiry process as adults preparing for baptism or affirmation of the baptismal covenant. In many cases, a parent or prospective parent may be considered a returning member or a searching member. (See p. 139.)

Church sponsors play a special role in listening for the parents' readiness or hesitation in deciding to have the child baptized. Reluctance to have the child baptized should be honored and explored. Going forward as if baptism were a mere formality should be carefully examined, and a faithful and mutual discernment made.

If the parents seem determined to defer baptism of the child until he or she is old enough to go through adult initiation, the child will remain a hearer and a constituent, but will not be baptized. The parents and godparents should receive ongoing support in the formation of the child, and the sponsors should seek to maintain a continuing relationship with the family as a sign of the care of God for them.

Note: If difficulty arises during the pregnancy or in the search for a child for adoption, the sponsors, godparents, and catechist are the primary ministers to the parents. If pregnancy is terminated by miscarriage, if the child is stillborn, if the prospective adoptee is not available, these persons continue to love and support the parents. They should notify the pastor of the situation.

When an expected child is born or adopted, appropriate notice and celebration will confirm a caring and growing relationship between the parents and the congregation. "An Order of Thanksgiving for the Birth or Adoption of a Child" (*The United Methodist Book of Worship*, 585-587) serves a specific way of sharing the family's joy and nurturing a sense of the congregation's welcome, prayer, and relationship to the family.

### Service One:
### Welcome of Children as Hearers Through the Parent(s)

In keeping with the practice of the church from the beginnings (see Acts 16:33), whole families have been baptized and made members of Christ. When parents have had adequate opportunity to test their readiness to sponsor their child for baptism, the congregation may welcome the child as a hearer using "A Service for Welcoming a Child As a Hearer" (see page 130). The pastor, catechist, and church sponsors have the critical task of impressing upon the parents that they are entering a time of formation and conversion for the purpose of reaffirming the baptismal covenant for themselves and finding God's guidance in forming the life of faith in the child. When a parent is becoming a hearer at the same time, appropriate adaptation of the service should be made.

Leaders should carefully guide and encourage the congregation to get to know and to pray for the families they have welcomed. Those who lead the congregation in prayers for the church and the world should include these families in their petitions. Sponsors should seek to introduce parents to others in the faith community.

### Stage Two:
### Preparation of the Parent(s) for Baptism of the Child

This stage invites exploration of prayer and worship, and understanding of the home as an extension of the people of God. Parents who have raised children in the congregation may be helpful in telling stories of how they raised their children and how the means of grace served to support them in the task of being parents.

Some families may enter the process of formation with "An Order of Thanksgiving for the Birth or Adoption of a Child" (See *The United Methodist Book of Worship*, 585-587). The first response of the congregation should always be welcome and joy as people seek the blessing of Christ. This act, whether in hospital, home, or church, is not tied to a parent's promises or commitment to the Christian faith. In using "An Order of Thanksgiving for the Birth or Adoption of Child," the congregation enacts God's unconditional love and blessing of the family and opens the door for further relationship and inquiry.

In larger congregations, formational groups specifically for expectant parents may be formed. In smaller congregations, expectant parents and parents participate in groups of adults preparing for baptism or for reaffirmation of the baptismal covenant. Church sponsors and godparents should also participate in the formational group sessions.

Formational groups, reflection on experience, prayer, ministry in daily life, and corporate worship are basic to this stage, as are exploration of the responsibilities that the parents and the godparents will assume at the baptism of the child. Some questions that can be useful in prompting reflection include these:

- What does your baptism mean to you? (Or if one or both parents are hearers, "What are you seeking that you also want for your child?")

- How can you model ministry and prayer for growing children?

- How can you introduce your child to the story of salvation?

- What is the role of godparents in faith development?

- How can you encourage your child's participation in worship?

- How is life in the family an extension of worship and keeping time with Christ?

- How can you tell your child the meaning of Holy Communion?

Because the next service in the process is "Calling Children to Baptism," reflection on the questions parents will be asked at the service of baptism is appropriate. See *The United Methodist Hymnal* (page 34, sections 4 and 5) or *The United Methodist Book of Worship* (page 88, sections 4 and 5). Reflection on the "Introduction to the Services of the Baptismal Covenant" in the Book of Worship, pages 81-85, will help participants to discover the life-long and ecumenical dimensions of baptism.

## SERVICE TWO: A SERVICE FOR CALLING CHILDREN TO BAPTISM

On an appropriate Sunday (preferably, the first Sunday in Lent or the first Sunday in Advent), children are presented for baptism along with adult hearers who are called to baptism. The date of the baptism is announced. During this service, parents of children who are called to baptism are questioned concerning their intention to be baptized or to reaffirm their baptismal vows and to take responsibility for sponsoring their child. The congregation reaffirms its support and offers its prayers for the children and their parental sponsors.

## STAGE THREE: PREPARATION FOR BAPTISM OF THE CHILD AND FOR THE RESPONSIBILITIES ACCEPTED AT BAPTISM

Assuming that this stage takes place during Lent or during Advent parents and their children will take part in the congregation's journey through the season. The worship and lectionary texts for both seasons are rich with imagery and clearly point the parents and children to Jesus. These texts form the basis for formational group reflection and family discussion.

Sponsors from the congregation and the catechist will continue to help the parents and godparents explore the responsibilities they will accept at baptism. Reflection on the lectionary texts can evoke consideration of the vision parents have for their children: What is your vision, your hope, for your child as a follower of Jesus? What does it mean to release and trust your child to God? What is the calling (vocation) and claim of God upon your child in baptism? How like Hannah or like Mary and Joseph are you? How are you different from them?

## SERVICE THREE: HOLY BAPTISM, THE BAPTISMAL COVENANT

On the announced day of the celebration of the baptismal covenant (preferably at the Easter Vigil, Easter Day, or the Baptism of the Lord), the candidates are baptized. *The United Methodist Hymnal* (33-43) and *The United Methodist Book of Worship* (86-99) provide the liturgical texts for Holy Baptism. Full Christian initiation, as reflected in "Services Of The Baptismal Covenant" includes water baptism, the laying on of hands, and Eucharist. Adequate planning for undiminished celebration of Easter and the entrance of the newly baptized into the way of eternal life is strongly encouraged. With infants and children, no less than adults, generous use of water, including immersion, is encouraged.

## STAGE FOUR:
## FORMATION OF THE CHILD IN FAITH AND DISCIPLESHIP

For infants and children the period following baptism is an extended combination of formation and integration (catechesis and mystagogy): formation in the Christian faith and life and exploration of how the sacraments of Baptism and Holy Communion are experienced as God's continuing call to conversion and ministry in daily life. During the developmental stages of infancy, childhood, early adolescence, and older adolescence, those baptized in infancy are guided in claiming the power of the symbols that celebrate their new life among the people of God. As their sense of self and their powers for self-direction grow, they need sponsors and guides who will help them discover the radical claim that Jesus, the Word of God, makes upon them. In adolescence the task of becoming hearers will be more sharply focused as they, the baptized, discover Christ's call to

❧ profession of faith in Christ and life-long discipleship;

❧ responsibility for the mission and ministry of the church;

❧ knowledge of the story and traditions of the church;

❧ discernment of their vocation and specific calling.

All of the formational and integrative processes of the adult stages of Christian initiation are part of this stage of Christian initiation when persons are baptized in infancy or early childhood.

Since this stage may last from a few years to as many as eighteen or twenty years and since parents, in partnership with the church, are long-term sponsors, there are many facets that contribute to faithful formation of the baptized. During this extended stage, the parents live out the baptismal covenant with their children. In the home and in church life, they encourage and model the life of faith and discipleship. Parents' full, active, and regular participation in worship and reception of Holy Communion with their children are the backbone of this extended period of growing faith.

Annual remembrance of the child's baptism and celebration with the godparents and congregational sponsors can help the growing child to know that an important event has already happened and continues to unfold and shape his or her life. If a baptismal candle was presented, lighting it and looking at pictures of the day of baptism can be ways of remembering the action of God and the presence of the church in a child's life.

Congregational acts of renewing the baptismal covenant on the Baptism of the Lord, at the Easter Vigil, on the Day of Pentecost, on All Saints Day, or at Watch Night, (see the Book of Worship, page 84) are opportunities for the growing child to rehearse and renew the covenant made at baptism.

The congregation's ministries of Christian education and nurture need the support and encouragement of the parents. Congregations must see such ministries as part of their essential ministry of welcoming, forming, and sending disciples. God's grace loving, calling, forgiving, empowering, and sending needs to be kept in focus so that children, as growing Christians, are listened to and involved in the love, work, and play of daily-life ministries.

Prayer and watchful care of the child as he or she approaches adolescence will help parents, godparents, and congregational leaders to discern his or her readiness to profess the faith and to affirm the baptismal covenant at confirmation. The pastor and the congregation's catechist are responsible for providing opportunities for the adolescent to focus the meaning of his or her journey to date and to prepare for profession of faith in Christ. With discernment of growing readiness to assume the disciplines of mature faith and responsibility for the baptismal covenant, sponsors for the young person should be chosen and should begin a mentor-apprentice relationship.

Church sponsors, the catechist, and the pastor support youth in focusing on questions such as these:

- As a baptized Christian, how will you endeavor to follow Jesus Christ under the guidance of the Holy Spirit?

- What is your sense of calling? How will you offer yourself as a living sacrifice in the community of Christ's followers and in the world? How is God calling you to ministry in daily life?

- What support will you need from other Christians in order to continue as Christ's faithful disciple? How has being in the formation group shaped your life? How is Christ calling you to participate in mutual support for faithful discipleship?

## SERVICE FOUR:
## SERVICE OF CONFIRMATION AND AFFIRMATION OF MINISTRY

On the Day of Pentecost, Transfiguration Sunday, or another appropriate Sunday in the Christian Year, youth and adults to be confirmed come forward and stand before or among the congregation. The services of the baptismal covenant in the hymnal and the Book of Worship provide the liturgical texts for confirmation. (See "Baptismal Covenant I," UMH, p. 33.) As part of the service, the confirmands, along with others affirming their ministry, may talk about specific forms of ministry or witness that they have begun or to which they feel called. The congregation offers prayers for them and celebrates the ministry of others who are reaffirming their discipleship.

Since profession of faith at confirmation and affirmation of ministry are not a stopping point or a graduation from a course of preparation, it is essential that the congregation provide settings and opportunities for ongoing support for discipleship and ministry in daily life. By this point in their growing discipleship, youth and adults who have just been confirmed will be accustomed to mutual accountability and to the grace of watching over one another in love. Confirmation must never be seen or allowed to be treated as arrival or as graduation from Christian growth and discipleship.

Small groups in which persons can continue to reflect on the Scriptures and daily experience and to watch over one another in love are essential for sustained participation in the essential ministry of the people of God. There are good reasons for youth to be part of groups of mixed ages, sexes, and levels of experience in Christian discipline.[71] Young disciples bring a freshness and directness that help older Christians to see and listen with new eyes. More experienced Christian disciples offer youth seasoned perspective and wisdom in use of the means of grace and in perseverance in the face of temptation and difficulty.

## A SERVICE FOR WELCOMING A CHILD AS A HEARER

*This service may be used during worship at any time of the year. The service is an adaptation of the one used for adults (p. 109). The primary difference is that the text here is appropriate for circumstances in which the congregation is welcoming a child as a hearer. In situations in which both adults and children are being welcomed as hearers during the same service, the presiding minister may make appropriate adjustments.*

*In a period of exploration guided by the catechist and/or the pastor and the sponsors, the parents develop clarity about what they desire of God for themselves and for the child they intend to present. This service should be used only when there is discernment that the parents seek life in Christ for themselves and for their children.*

*This service is designed to be used within a service of worship. The sponsor, the parent(s) and the child to be presented gather outside the church or in the entry area. When the presiding minister has given an introduction about what is about to take place, the congregation may sing an appropriate song, psalm or hymn as the people turn toward the place of welcome. The presiding and assisting ministers move to the place where those to be presented are assembled. This service of welcome invites adaptation, especially at the Greeting [1] and Opening Dialogue [3]. In adapting the service, the presiding minister should maintain brevity and focus while seeking to embody the hospitality and welcome of the gospel.*

*This service may be used following the sermon. In such cases, the Invitation to Hear the Word of God [7] should be omitted.*

*For simplicity, the text of the service is oriented to welcome one child. It is assumed that two parents and one sponsor present the child for baptism. The service can easily be changed if more or fewer people are involved.*

1. **Greeting**

   *The pastor stands before the parents and child and greets them in a warm and hospitable way. Addressing them, the sponsor, and the congregation, the presider expresses the joy and delight of the church in welcoming persons who are drawn to the story of Jesus and to the life of faith. The presider or another congregational leader welcomes the family with words and gestures that invite them to come and stand before the people. As they come before the congregation, all may join in singing an appropriate hymn, song, or psalm.*

2. **Presentation**

   *The sponsor, standing with the parents and the child to be presented, makes the appropriate presentation:*

   I present the _____ (*family name*) family who desires this child,
   _____ (*child's name*), to know and follow Christ.

3. **Opening Dialogue**
   *When the family has been presented, the presider addresses the parents by name, asking:*

   _____ *(parents' first names), what do you seek for your child?*
   *The parents answer to the presider and the people with one of the following or another appropriate response:*
   **I seek life in Jesus Christ for my child.**
   or
   **I seek, for my child, to know Jesus Christ.**
   *The presider has the option of asking other questions about the desires and intentions of the parents). Particular stories or experiences that have brought the parents to this step on the journey of faith may be told.*

4. **First Acceptance of the Gospel Through the Parents**
   *The catechist addresses the parents:*
   Jesus said, "I am the light of the world. Whoever follows me
   will never walk in darkness but will have the light of life."
   You have been drawn to Christ's light,
   and you desire light and life for your child.
   Journey with us and learn to trust Christ.
   Grow with your child to believe in Christ with all your heart.
   Jesus will show you how to love God and to love your neighbor,
   and will lead you in guiding your child to do the same.

   Are you ready, with the help of God, to sponsor your child in the life in Christ?
   **I am.**
   Will you be faithful in attending the worship of God, hearing the Word of God, and leading your child to do the same?
   **I will.**
   Will you listen to the Word of God and open your heart and mind to Jesus as you guide your child to welcome him as Lord and Savior?
   **I will, with God's help.**

5. **Commitment of Sponsors and Congregation**
   *The catechist says to sponsor and to the entire congregation:*
   Will you care for *these parents* with your prayer and companionship?
   Will you walk with *them* as they guide this child in the way that leads to life?
   **We will.**

   *The sponsor places a hand on the shoulder of the child and the parents, while the presider says:*
   The Lord be with you.
   **And also with you.**

   Let us pray.
   Almighty God, like a shepherd searching for lost sheep

and like a parent waiting to welcome home a wandering child,
you reach out and draw this child, _____ (*child's name*),
to the waters of baptism.
You welcome _____ (*child's name*)
to the journey of grace and new birth.
You welcome *him/her* through *his/her parents* and sponsor,
who today declare their desire for this child
to live the way of love and life through dying and rising with Jesus.
Today, through *these parents,* we welcome this child
as a hearer of the Word of God.
We bless you and praise you for what you are doing among us. **Amen.**

*All may sing an appropriate hymn, song, or psalm.*
*Suggestions from UMBOW:* "Sing to the Lord a New Song" (181); "May the
Warm Winds of Heaven" (198 or 200); "Tino tenda Jesu (Thank You Jesus,)"
(203)

6. **Marking with the Sign of the Cross**
*The sponsor traces the cross on the forehead of the hearer, the child, as the*
*presider addresses the hearer:*
Receive the mark of the cross on your forehead,
as a sign of the way you are to follow,
and as a sign of Christ with you in strength and love.
May the power of the Holy Spirit enable you to know
and to follow our Lord, Jesus Christ.
**Amen.**

*Marking with the sign of the cross may be expanded to include other parts of the*
*body using [6A] on p. 111.*

*The people may respond, saying or singing:*
**Glory and praise to you, Almighty God.**
*Or the congregation may sing an appropriate hymn, song, or psalm.*
*Suggestion from UMH "I Want to Walk as a Child of the Light" (206)*

7. **Invitation to Come and Hear the Word of God**
*A reader for the day's service invites the new hearer and his/her parents to hear*
*the word of God using these or similar words:*
God's word is like bread for our hearts; we cannot live without it.
God's word is like rain that comes down upon the earth,
bringing forth fruit in our lives.
Come and be with us as a hearer of the Word of God.
Let the Word of God guide your way and bring you to everlasting life.

*Here the sponsor may present a Bible to the hearer, placing the hand of the child on the Bible as the catechist says:*

> Receive the good news of Jesus Christ, the Son of God.
> Hear the gospel and listen for the voice of Jesus, the living Lord.
> Grow to hear, trust, and follow him.

*The hearer, parents and sponsor are seated. The worship continues with the readings of Scripture and the sermon, except when the service for welcoming a child as a hearer is used following the sermon. When it is used following the sermon, the worship continues with the Concerns and Prayers, which include prayers for the hearer.*

✝

## A SERVICE FOR CALLING CHILDREN TO BAPTISM, THROUGH THEIR PARENTS

*This service is normally used on the first Sunday in Lent. When persons are being prepared for baptism at the Baptism of the Lord, it is used on the first Sunday of Advent.*

*The service presupposes that parents presenting their child to be called as a candidate for baptism 1) are undergoing their own continuing conversion and formation in the Christian way of love and faith and 2) are either professing members of the church or in the process of becoming professing members. Appropriate conferences and discernment of readiness by those who have worked with the parents must precede the service so that any hint of mere formality is avoided.*

*The sermon should be appropriate to the situation and should address the congregation, the hearers, and the parents and call them to journey in prayer and discipline together.*

*The service follows the sermon. During a hymn of response, the hearers, parents, their sponsor, and the catechist come forward and stand before the assembly and the presiding minister.*

*Since this is an occasion on which hearers, both adults and children, may be called to baptism, the service used for adults has been adopted here for calling children through their parents. If only adults are being called to baptism, "A Service For Calling Persons To Baptism" on p. 113 should be used.*

✝

### 1. Presentation

*With the hearers who are to be presented facing the people, the catechist addresses the presider and the congregation:*

> Dear friends in Christ, _____ (*names of adult hearers*), and
> _____, (*names of child hearers*), through their *parents*, have
> been hearing the Word of God with us.
> *They have* been sharing in our way of life in Jesus Christ.
> We have given *them* our support

with friendship, prayer, and example.
God's transforming grace has been at work among us and in *them.*
*Easter* is drawing near, and *Lent* is a time of preparation for those who ask to
participate in the sacraments.
Let us hear of their journey and of God's call to Holy Baptism.

*When the date of baptism will be at a service other than the Easter Vigil or
Easter, the leader may substitute other appropriate words, such as "The Baptism
of the Lord is drawing near, and Advent is a time of preparation for those who
ask to participate in the sacraments."*

## 2. Affirmation by Sponsors

*The presider, speaking to the sponsors, says:*
_____ (*name of adult hearers*) seek initiation into Christ's
holy church. The _____ (*family name*) family seeks initiation
of their (*child*) _____ (*names of children*), into Christ's holy
church. We want to know that the adult hearers are truly called to enter this
life in Christ through Holy Baptism. We want to know that the parents of the
child are called to present *him/her* for Holy Baptism.
You have walked with *them* on a journey of conversion.
You have prayed for *them* to know the voice of Christ
and to know that *their* daily life is a participation
in the story of his life, death, and resurrection.
As God is your witness, tell us of *their* readiness
to obey Christ's call in the baptismal covenant.

*The presider says to the sponsors:*
*Have they* faithfully joined in the worship of God?
**They have.**
*Have they* heard God's word and walked in the light of Jesus in their daily life?
**They have.**
*Have they* come to know Christ's story and way, and *have they* engaged in
ministry with the poor and neglected?
**They have.**

*Here each sponsor may speak in a brief and focused way of the growth and
courage of the hearers or their parents in learning the Christian life. The affirmation should be expressed in words that witness to God's gracious work in their
hearts and actions. Each sponsor's witness should express God's love and should
neither praise them nor to expose or embarrass them.*

*The presider says to the congregation:*
My brothers and sisters, you have heard the witness
concerning *the hearers and parents.*
Will you support *these* persons as candidates for baptism

and continue to support *them and their families*
with your prayers and loving actions,
as we journey toward *Easter* and the waters of baptism?
**With glad and expectant hearts, we will!**

## 3. Invitation and Call

*The presider says to the hearers and the parents:*
You have heard the affirmation made by your *sponsors*
and the promise of love from the people of God.
You have heard the call of Jesus and we ask you to answer clearly.

*The presider to the adult hearers:*
Do you desire to be called to initiation and to be baptized at Easter?
**I do.**

*or to the parents:*
Do you desire for your child to be called to initiation
and to be baptized at *Easter?*
**I do.**

## 4. Declaration and Charge

*The presider, taking the right hand of each hearer, says:*
_____ *(name),* in the name Jesus Christ, we call you to life in
the church and to initiation into the mystery of Jesus' death and resurrection
through baptism at the *Easter Vigil (Easter or the Baptism of the Lord).*

*Each candidate or the parents and the sponsor respond:*
**Thanks be to God!**

*When each candidate has been called to baptism, the presider assures the adult
candidates and the parents of children of God's faithfulness and encourages
them with these or similar words:*
You are learning to trust God with your life.
God is faithful and will complete the work that God has begun in you.
May God illumine and strengthen you with grace
until sin has no more dominion over you.
May grace make you instruments of righteousness and praise to our God.
Now you are called to enter, with courage and faith, into a *forty day* retreat.
With us, follow Jesus into the truth and life of the gospel
*at the festival of his death and resurrection*
[or, *at the festival of his baptism,* or other appropriate words].

*Then the presider turns to the sponsors and charges them saying:*
You have spoken with favor concerning the
*candidates* for baptism *and the parents.*
Receive *them* as chosen in the Lord and

support *them* in keeping the disciplines of prayer, fasting,
meditation on the Word of God, and examination of conscience.
Share with *them* the risk of full conversion.

**5. Concerns and Prayers**

*The newly-called candidates, the parents, and sponsors remain together before
the congregation so that they may be included in the congregation's Concerns
and Prayers. If the candidates are to leave for reflection on Scripture, "Prayer
over the Candidates" [6] may take place here with the Concerns and Prayers [5]
following the departure of the candidates and their sponsors.*

**6. Prayer Over the Candidates**

*The sponsors and the parents each place a hand on the shoulder of the candi-
dates, and the presider extends hands over them praying:*

The Lord be with you.
**And also with you.**
Let us pray:
God of love and power,
your purpose is to bring all creation within your saving embrace.
Draw into Christ's life *these people,* whom you have chosen.
By the power of your Spirit bring *them to be true sons and daughters*
of the gospel and adopt *them* by the mystery of your grace
through Christ, our Lord.
**Amen.**

*Here the candidates, the parents, and their sponsors return to their seats or go to
a place for the meeting of their formational group. If they leave the service, they
should be sent forth with a blessing and a call to hear the Word of God. The service continues to its conclusion.*

✝

## HOLY BAPTISM: THE BAPTISMAL COVENANT

*Since the services of the Baptismal Covenant are readily available in the hymnal
and the Book of Worship, they are not printed here. "The Baptismal Covenant I," pp.
33-39 in* The United Methodist Hymnal *and pp. 86-94 in* The United Methodist
Book of Worship, *is the appropriate service to use for baptism when there are both
persons who can answer for themselves and those who cannot. When only children
and others unable to answer for themselves are to be baptized, "Baptismal Covenant
II" (UMH, pp. 39-43; UMBOW, pp. 95-99) should be used. Full initiation includes
baptism, the laying on of hands, and the Eucharist.*

*When baptism occurs at the Easter Vigil, the resources of* The United Methodist
Book of Worship, *369-376, should be used in planning and leading the service.*

*When baptism occurs on Baptism of the Lord, baptism should follow the service of the Word. The United Methodist Book of Worship, 299-301, provides specific resources for use at the Baptism of the Lord.*

*Generous use of water, anointing with oil, and high celebration of the Eucharist, are encouraged. Strong sacramental action will serve to build strong faith and a memorable initiation into Christ and the church.*

## A Service of Confirmation
## and Affirmation of Ministry in Daily Life

*"Baptismal Covenant I" is the appropriate service to use with those baptized in infancy or childhood who are now ready to profess their faith in Christ and to be confirmed. People ready to be confirmed have persevered through an extended period of formation and conversion during adolescence or young adulthood. In this service, God offers such persons an opportunity, within the context of the baptismal covenant, to remember and confirm their baptism and to affirm their commitment to a life of discipleship and ministry to which God continues to call and nourish them in the Eucharist.*

*In this service, the congregation recognizes and celebrates the witness and ministry of persons baptized as children and rejoices as they make their own profession of faith and commitment to a life of discipleship. While special focus is given to their commitment, the service may be planned to include youth and adults who are recently baptized or returning to life in communion with all the baptized. Congregational reaffirmation of the baptismal covenant is also encouraged. Such a service can be a powerful witness and celebration of the grace of God, working in all of the people; those planning the service will need to take into account its scope.*

*When baptism occurs at Easter, this service is appropriately incorporated into worship on the Day of Pentecost. When baptism occurs on the Baptism of the Lord, this service is appropriately included in worship on Transfiguration Sunday. When baptism occurs at some other time during the year, this service can be included in worship on a day that focuses on the work of the Holy Spirit or the witness of the Church in daily service to God and neighbor.*

*Those to be confirmed, along with persons recently baptized and those reaffirming the baptismal covenant, may be invited to respond to a question such as this: Having determined to follow Jesus in daily witness and service, how will you endeavor to follow Jesus under the guidance of the Holy Spirit? (See the second rubric under section 3 in* The United Methodist Book of Worship, 87.)

*Careful planning of the service will prevent this from being hurried. The sermon should be brief and appropriate to affirmation of the ministry the people of God.*

# Chapter Three

# SERVICES FOR PERSONS RETURNING TO THE BAPTISMAL COVENANT

## INTRODUCTION

When persons have been baptized and have subsequently lived outside the communion of the Church, they are separated members. They may fall within three basic categories:

❧ those baptized as children, but never formed and integrated into the life and discipline of the faith community;

❧ those baptized and minimally formed, who have drifted away from the Church;

❧ those baptized, formed as disciples, and incorporated into the body of Christ, who at some time chose to depart from the baptismal covenant for reasons including adherence to a non-Christian religion or way of life, rejection of the faith and ministry of the church, or a sense of rejection or lack of care by the church.

When such persons are drawn again to Christ and the church, they are returning members; the grace of God offered to them in the baptismal covenant has never been withdrawn.

## A SET OF STAGES AND SERVICES PARALLEL TO THOSE FOR UNBAPTIZED ADULTS

The set of stages and services used with returning members parallels the stages and services used with adults in the initiation process. It is designed to restore and reconcile baptized adults, including mature youth, who have lived apart from the church. While these persons have already been baptized, they have not experienced the fullness of conversion, formation, and participation in the faith and ministry of the Christian community; or they may be persons who have lapsed in professing the Christian faith in word and deed. Like the unbaptized, those seeking to reaffirm the baptismal covenant may come with a variety of experiences and needs. Some may have no experience of the church, except baptism. Some may have fallen away from even a nominal practice of faithful discipleship. Some may have been deeply wounded by a past experience related to the church. Some may come with little knowledge of the way of faith. Others may come with sophisticated knowledge, but little experience, of faith and the means of grace.

## SEARCHING MEMBERS

Some persons who are active participants in the life of the congregation may find that they want to go deeper in their journey of faith. In fact, in a congregation in which there is a recovery of vital faith practiced in worship, small groups, and ministry in daily life, it is expected that many persons will seek a deeper experience of knowing God in Christ by the power of the Holy Spirit. They are not returning members. They are searching members. Searching members may be appropriately included in the processes outlined for returning members.

Pastors and catechists should make appropriate adaptations for the participation of searching members. Leaders should be alert to the needs they may have for acts of penitence and restoration. Gracious and in-depth listening will be necessary to discern the degree of repentance and restoration needed by a searching member. The work of the Holy Spirit in bringing a member to such a search should be respected and honored by the congregation and its spiritual leaders. If the searching member has expressed a need for a journey toward a deeper faith, it is not recommended that he or she serve as a sponsor for another person while going through the process.

The primary level of participation for searching members should be in the progressive stages of the processes of Christian initiation. Most will not need to participate in the services, except for "Reaffirmation of the Baptismal Covenant" and "Affirmation of Ministry."

## SERVICES USED WITH RETURNING MEMBERS

Since they are baptized, returning members are not to be treated as hearers and candidates for baptism. This set of stages and services faces a double challenge of faithful recognition of God's gracious covenant made in baptism, on the one hand, and the essential human response of conversion and faith, on the other. The services provided for those preparing to affirm the baptismal covenant are distinctly different from the services for persons who have not yet been baptized. Care should be taken throughout the stages and services to underscore that these persons are members of the body of Christ through baptism. Prayers offered in meetings and in worship should acknowledge their baptism, while supporting their penitence and conversion.

In some congregations, where size and resources are adequate, a separate track of small group meetings and preparation may be desirable. In other congregations, where resources are more limited, those coming to the waters of baptism and those returning to affirm their baptismal covenant may attend meetings together during each stage of Christian initiation.

There are four stages of preparation and formation, each followed by a service of transition. Throughout the process, returning members are valued by the community as examples of the need of all the faithful to reexamine and renew their baptismal covenant. Returning members serve as models and prophetic reminders of the need for continuing conversion.

The logic of the Lent-Holy Week-Easter portion of the calendar is evangelical. It is so geared to conversion and to God's restoration and reconciliation of human beings that the services that follow (with exception of "Service One: Inquiry") are directly tied to Ash Wednesday, Holy Thursday, and Easter Vigil or Easter Day. Congregations who find it necessary to call returning members to conversion, celebrate reconciliation, and reaffirm the baptismal covenant at another time of the year will need to make thoughtful adaptation of the stages and services that follow.

## COMMENTARY ON THE STAGES AND SERVICES

### STAGE ONE: INQUIRY

The stage of inquiring is designed for telling stories and giving baptized inquirers information about the Christian way and the life of the local congregation. The aim is to create a hospitable setting in which returning members may determine whether or not they desire to enter a disciplined period of mature formation in the story of God's saving work and through experiences in worship, prayer, and service. One or more sponsors are chosen from the congregation for each baptized inquirer.

The focal questions that sponsors, the pastor, and the catechist will help inquirers to struggle with are these: What place do God and faith have in your life? What does it mean that you have been baptized? What are your deep desires for God? Are you ready to reorder your life through worship, prayer, reflection on Scripture, community life, and ministry in order to hear and follow the call of God in Jesus Christ?

This stage ends with the service of welcome for returning members. The service may be planned for any Lord's Day that an inquirer within the community determines is appropriate for his or her spiritual journey. Reaching that determination should take place in prayer and discernment with the sponsor, catechist, and pastor.

### SERVICE ONE: WELCOMING A RETURNING MEMBER

During the service, the baptized inquirers are presented as persons who are already members of the body of Christ through the sacrament of baptism. They are welcomed to a process of repentance and growth in the faith community. They are asked questions that lead into the next stage and are prayed for by the whole congregation. "A Celebration of New Beginnings in Faith" (*The United Methodist Book of Worship*, 588) may serve as an alternative to "A Service for Welcoming a Returning Member" (p. 144) if appropriate references to baptism are included in the service and particularly when the person is a searching member.

Some may question the need for public welcome of returning members. While it is true that lapsed members may return to life in the church at any time, there are strong reasons for intentional and public reintegration of returning members. Separated members, who simply return, can quietly and gradually find their rightful place in the community of faith. The disadvantage to this way of returning is that they do so in privacy and obscurity, and the congregation misses the opportunity to do the evangelical work of reconciling and restoring them to vital life in the church.

"A Service for Welcoming a Returning Member" should not be used to receive professing members who are transferring from another congregation or denomination, or a searching member, since in both cases the person is not returning to life within the baptismal covenant.

## STAGE TWO: FORMATION IN FAITH AND MINISTRY

This period will be as long as it is needed by the returning member. Some persons will not have had formation in Christian faith and life and will need extended time in seeking God and in discovering the meaning of life within the baptismal covenant. Others will have had enough formation to move to the next stage quickly. Discernment of readiness will be made by the returning member, the sponsor, and the catechist.

In this stage, returning members, along with sponsors, catechists, and others in the congregation, engage in deeper exploration of the story of salvation, worship, prayer, and ministry in daily life. The lectionary passages (or some other plan of Scripture reading) used in worship will be the basis of group conversation. The baptized explore the meaning of their baptism and seek to discern their call and gifts for service. They experience a pattern of accountability in which they are supported by other believers. In practicing the basics of worship, devotion, justice, and compassion, they experience the Christian life lived in community. Other members of the congregation may be called upon to help returning members discover the basics of Christian life and witness. Significant time is spent in service to the poor and in other social ministries. Reflecting theologically on ministry allows them to discern the voice of God in daily life and to be formed by the call to witness and service.

The connection between what the risen Lord is doing and what is needed in the various settings of daily life is a primary focus in this and all of the stages of Christian initiation. Weekly reflection in formational groups should focus on the connections between faith and life in the areas of family, leisure, work, community, church, and national and global concerns. Attention should be given to questions such as these: Who is there? What is going on? What is needed? Where do you see God at work? When hearers are invited to reflect on and to discuss such questions, they find ways to talk about their stories and their ministry in daily life.

There are no clear guidelines for whether or not a returning member should participate in Holy Communion. Baptized members have a place at the table. However, a returning member may have reservations about sharing in the eucharistic meal if he or she has been alienated from the church or has a sense of not yet being ready for the meal. Wise pastors and sponsors will acknowledge the reservations and discern the roots of the misgiving. In some cases, waiting until Holy Thursday to partake of Communion may be a powerful witness to the reconciling dimension of the sacrament. However, that approach should not be the rule.

## SERVICE TWO: CALLING THE BAPTIZED TO CONTINUING CONVERSION

This service is used on Ash Wednesday. Returning members who have been preparing to return to life within the baptismal covenant are presented to the congregation. The members of the church promise to support them within the patterns, discipline, and love of the community. In turn, the faithful are reminded of their own unfaithfulness and their need for repentance and conversion. Sponsors witness to the growing faithfulness and discipline of the returning members. Together the faithful and the returning members receive the mark of the cross with the imposition of ashes and the call to repentance and return.

## STAGE THREE: IMMEDIATE PREPARATIONS FOR AFFIRMATION OF THE BAPTISMAL COVENANT

This stage leads directly to the affirmation of the baptismal covenant at the Easter Vigil. In the group meetings, returning members continue to talk about their ongoing experience of conversion. The focus continues to be upon deepening disciplines; consistent use of the means of grace; conversion; and participation in worship, prayer, and ministry.

The lectionary provides the material for reflection on life in relationship to Jesus, the living Lord. During this stage, there is emphasis on what must die in order for the life-transforming power of Jesus to burst forth in daily life. By reflecting on the renunciation of evil and the profession of faith in the baptismal covenant service (UMH, p. 34, section 4), returning members are encouraged to discover God's transforming grace and to become in daily life what Christ has made them in baptism, part of God's new creation.

During this phase, a retreat, vigil, or weekend experience may be held to intensify their repentance and self-giving in faith and to allow the congregation an opportunity to show its support and love.

"A Celebration of Reconciliation," page 148, should be included in the Holy Thursday liturgy (UMBOW, 351-354). The service powerfully enacts confession, forgiveness, and reconciliation. Reconciliation and absolution are acted out in the footwashing. The peace seals the restoration and reconciliation as the returning members share the eucharistic meal with the congregation.

## SERVICE THREE: AFFIRMATION OF THE BAPTISMAL COVENANT

During the Easter Vigil (UMBOW, 369-376) and following any baptisms in the church the returning and searching members reaffirm the baptismal covenant, as the whole congregation celebrates its death, burial, and resurrection with Christ. If the returning members have not previously affirmed the baptismal covenant, they are confirmed. Those who have previously affirmed the baptismal covenant reaffirm it now with the whole congregation.

## STAGE FOUR: CALL TO MISSION
## AND REFLECTION ON THE SACRAMENTS

Following confirmation or reaffirmation of the baptismal covenant, it is appropriate for returning members to join with the newly baptized in exploring how the sacraments of Baptism and Holy Communion are experienced as God's continuing call to ministry and witness in daily living. Sponsors and the catechist continue to support members by focusing on these questions:

- ❧ As a baptized, communing Christian, how will you endeavor to follow Jesus Christ under the guidance of the Holy Spirit?

- ❧ What is your sense of your calling? How will your life be offered as a living sacrifice in the community of Christ's royal priesthood and in the world? How is God calling you to ministry in daily life?

- ❧ What support will you need from other Christians in order to persevere as Christ's faithful disciple? How has being in the formation group shaped your life? How is Christ calling you to participate in mutual support for faithful discipleship?

The lectionary readings will provide material for discussion and reflection.

Since returned members have been restored to the community of the faithful, Sunday worship during the Great Fifty Days should emphasize their interaction with the congregation. Joyful celebration and settings for informal conversation should be planned.

## SERVICE FOUR: A SERVICE FOR AFFIRMATION OF MINISTRY

On the Day of Pentecost or another day when "A Service for Affirmation of Ministry" is used, it is appropriate for returned members to tell about their sense of the ministry to which Jesus is calling them. This service is more fully described on pages 120-121.

## SERVICES FOR MEMBERS RETURNING TO THE BAPTISMAL COVENANT

### A SERVICE FOR WELCOMING A RETURNING MEMBER

*This service welcomes baptized adults who have been living outside of the communion of the church and have now begun a journey of inquiry about the life of faith. The service allows the congregation to welcome persons who are ready to begin the journey and to promise its companionship for them.*

*This service may be used in worship at any time of the year as long as the congregation is present. It should be scheduled when the returning member is ready to be welcomed into the journey of life within the baptismal covenant. In order to avoid confusion, the service should not be used on the same day that the congregation welcomes an unbaptized person as a hearer.*

*Only the Welcome [5] needs to be printed for the congregation.*

*Careful pastoral preparation will insure that this service is not* pro forma. *The inquiry stage that precedes the service aims at helping the person to discover what he or she most desires of God and how to answer the first question in the service.*

*The service is worded for the welcome of one person. The language can be easily adapted for use when welcoming more than one person.*

*The service may take place after the opening hymn and greeting. The presiding minister may include in the greeting expressions of the joy of the church in welcoming the returning member and a reminder that the inquirer is already baptized. When appropriate, the presider or catechist may tell briefly about the spiritual journey that brings this person to return to life in communion with the church.*

**1. Presentation**

*The sponsor brings the baptized inquirer before the people and presents him or her to the congregation, saying:*

I present _____ (name), who desires to return to the way of Christ in communion with the church.

*The presider addresses the inquirer, who faces the people, and asks:*

What do you seek?

*The returning member answers with one of the following or another appropriate response:*

**I seek restoration of my life to Christ and his people.**
*or*
**I seek a new beginning in faith**

*The presider then continues:*

In baptism, we were united with Christ in his death and resurrection.

With you, we were made members of Christ's body, the Church. With you, we have been called to know the fellowship of his sufferings and the power of his resurrection. Now come to discover the meaning of your baptism and your place among the people of God.

**2. Declaration of Intent**

The presider questions the returning member:

Will you explore the vows made at baptism, and strive to keep them in the fellowship of this congregation of Christ's Church?

**I will.**

Will you attend worship regularly to hear God's word?

**I will.**

Will you join us in our life of service to the poor and lonely?

**I will.**

Will you seek to know the gifts God has given you and to discern how they are to be used in bringing the reign of God's justice and peace to daily life?

**I will.**

**3. Charge to the Sponsor and Congregation**

*The presider addressing the sponsor says:*

You have been chosen to serve as a companion for _____ (*name*). Will you walk with and support *him/her* on the journey of conversion; and will you, by example and prayer, help *him/her* to grow in loving God and loving neighbor?

**I will.**

*The presider addressing the congregation says:*

Will all of you who witness this new beginning keep _____ (*name*) in your prayers and help *him/her* to know Jesus Christ, welcome *him/her* into your lives, and encourage *him/her* until *he/she* is established in communion with Christ's Church?

**We will.**

**4. Blessing of the Returning Member**

*The returning member remains standing, and the sponsor places a hand on his/her shoulder. The pastor, extending hands toward the returning member, blesses him/her with these or similar words:*

_____ (*name*), you are a child of God,
a servant of Christ, and a temple of the Holy Spirit.
You were reborn in the water of baptism
and made to share in Christ's royal priesthood.
You are one with us in Christ Jesus.
May almighty God bless you and keep you in eternal life.

**Amen.**

## 5. Welcome

*The presider, addressing the congregation, says:*
Please welcome _____ (*name*) among you.

*The people respond, speaking to the returning member:*
**We thank God that you are one with us in the household of God.**
**Confess with us the faith of Christ crucified,**
**proclaim his resurrection,**
**and walk with us in his way of discipleship.**

*The catechist or other representative of the congregation may present a Bible to the returning member, saying:*
Receive the good news of Jesus Christ, the Son of God.
Read and listen for the voice of Jesus, the living Lord.
Grow to hear, trust, and follow him.

*The service continues with an act of praise or the prayer for illumination and the reading of the Scripture.*

*The returning member may be prayed for in the Concerns and Prayers.*

*At the Peace and at the close of the service, an opportunity for the returning member and the community to greet one another will strengthen the enactment of welcome.*

*Depending on circumstances and the congregation's style, "A Celebration of New Beginnings in Faith" (UMBOW, 588) may be more suitable, particularly if the person is a professing member and is searching for a deeper faith (see p. 139). If "A Celebration of New Beginnings in Faith" is used, several parts of "A Service for Welcoming a Returning Member" should be included:*
 *(a) the question, "What do you seek?" [1]*
 *(b) a question or questions that ask if the person will share in worship, prayer, reflection on the Scriptures, and service[2]*
 *(c) substitution of the adapted form of the Blessing [4]*

✝

## CALLING THE BAPTIZED TO CONTINUING CONVERSION

*When returning members seek the way of penitence and restoration to the communion of the church at Easter, this service is designed to be included within the Ash Wednesday liturgy (see UMBOW, 321-324).*

*In place of the "Invitation to the Observation of Lenten Discipline"(UMBOW, 322) the words and actions that follow may be used:*

> Dear brothers and sisters in Christ,
> each year we observe with great devotion
> the days of our Lord's passion and resurrection;
> and it is the practice of Christians that before the Easter celebration,
> there be a forty-day season of spiritual preparation.
> During this season, converts to the faith are prepared for Holy Baptism.
> It is also a time when persons who
> have been separated from the community of faith
> may be reconciled by penitence and forgiveness
> and be restored to the covenant they entered at their baptism.
> In this way, the whole congregation is reminded
> of the mercy and forgiveness proclaimed in the gospel of Jesus Christ
> and the need we all have to renew our faith.

*Here the returning members are presented individually. Each sponsor says:*

> I present _____ (name) who desires to journey with us by self-examination and repentance and to be restored to the way of Christ. *He/she* is ready to join us as we give ourselves to Christ during these forty days.

*Then the presider addresses the whole assembly saying:*

> I invite you, therefore, in the name of the Church,
> to observe a holy Lent
> by self examination and repentance;
> by prayer, fasting, and self-denial;
> and by reading and meditating on God's Holy Word.
> To make a right beginning of repentance,
> and as a mark of our mortal nature,
> let us now kneel before our Creator and Redeemer.

*A brief silence is kept, the congregation seated or kneeling.*

*The presider then follows the service on page 323 of The United Methodist Book of Worship, starting with the "Thanksgiving Over the Ashes." The presider may invite the returning members to be the first ones to come forward and to receive the sign of the cross with ashes. The presider will say to them:*

> The Holy Spirit work within you
> that having been born of water and the Spirit,
> you may be a living sign of the conversion
> and mercy to which the Lord calls all of us.

*The returning members rise and join the presider in applying the ashes to the rest of the people.*

*The service continues with the Confession and Pardon (UMBOW , p. 323).*

+

## CELEBRATION OF RECONCILIATION ON HOLY THURSDAY

*The steps taken in the services above, "Welcoming a Returning Member" and "Calling the Baptized to Continuing Conversion," lead to this celebration. In this service of public reconciliation, returning members and the congregation celebrate openly the restoration of their life together as the people of God.*

*This service is designed to be included in "A Service of Worship for Holy Thursday Evening" (UMBOW, 351-354). It is designed for use when there are baptized persons seeking to return to communion within the baptismal covenant at Easter. The Holy Thursday worship may be adapted as follows:*

(1) *The Confession and Pardon (UMBOW, 352) is not used at the beginning of the service since it will be included just before the footwashing.*

(2) *The Concerns and Prayers may be incorporated into The Great Thanksgiving (UMBOW, 64-65) at the end of the section that begins "Pour out your Spirit . . ."*

*After the sermon, the presider may address the assembly with these or similar words:*[72]

Fellow servants of our Lord Jesus Christ,
on the night before his death,
Jesus set an example for his disciples
by washing their feet, an act of humble service.
He taught that strength and growth
in the life of the kingdom (*reign*) of God
come not by power, authority, or even miracle,
but by such lowly service.

He also taught
that those who would continue as his disciples
must accept such service from one another,
and be restored to the peace and purity of their baptism.

Therefore, I invite you
who seek to be restored to the way of Christ
and who share in his royal priesthood through baptism,
to come forward,
that I may recall whose servant I am
by following the example of my Master.
But come remembering his admonition
that what will be done for you
is also to be done by you to others,
for "servants are not greater than their master,
nor are messengers greater than the one who sent them.
If you know these things, you are blessed if you do them."

*The returning members come forward and kneel before the presider who speaks to them:*

    My friends in Christ,
    the steadfast love of the Lord is unending,
    and God's mercy is unending.
    Jesus welcomes sinners to his table.
    May God, who purifies our hearts,
    help you to confess your sins
    and receive God's pardon.
    Your return reminds us of our unfaithfulness and sin.
    With you, we confess our broken promises and our need of grace.

*A setting of "O Lamb of God" may be sung.*
*Here the returning members and the faithful join in the Confession and Pardon*

    **Most merciful God,**
    **we your Church confess**
    **that often our Spirit has not been that of Christ.**
    **Where we have failed to love one another as he loves us,**
    **where we have pledged loyalty to him with our lips**
    **and then betrayed, deserted, or denied him,**
    **forgive us, we pray;**
    **and by your Spirit make us faithful in every time of trial;**
    **through Jesus Christ our Lord. Amen.**[73]

*The presider then asks the returning members:*[74]
    Do you turn again to Christ?
        **I do.**
    Do you forgive those who have sinned against you?
        **I forgive them.**

    Who is in a position to condemn? Only Christ.
    But Christ suffered and died for us,
    was raised from the dead and ascended on high for us,
    and continues to intercede for us.
    Believe the good news!

*Here the faithful join the presider in proclaiming forgiveness to the returning members:*
    **In the name of Jesus Christ, you are forgiven!**

*Then the presider takes a place among the faithful while the returning members rise and face the people, saying to them:*
    In the name of Jesus Christ you are forgiven!

*All the people respond:*
**Glory to God. Amen.**

*The service continues with footwashing (UMBOW, 351 and 353) following this order announced by the presider:*
    *The presider washes the feet of the returning members;*
    *then the rest of the people are invited to come forward;*
    *and the presider, assisted by the returning members, washes their feet.*

*Others may be invited to assist in the footwashing if the numbers of people are too great.*

*Following the washing of feet, the service may continue with The Peace (UMBOW, 353).*

## ✝
## THE BAPTISMAL COVENANT: REAFFIRMATION

See Commentary on the Stages and Services for Members Returning to the Baptismal Covenant, p. 142.

## ✝
## A SERVICE FOR AFFIRMATION OF MINISTRY IN DAILY LIFE

See pages 120-121.

# Word List (Glossary)

This list includes basic words and terms of Christian initiation. Words in italics are technical terms and were used in the catechumenate of the ancient church. Other words are terms basic to the processes of Christian initiation as they are used in this book. An asterisk indicates both an ancient and contemporary usage.

**Candidate for Baptism:** A person who has been called to baptism following a period of being a hearer. Persons are candidates during the third stage of Christian initiation, usually during the weeks of Lent or Advent. The term is sometimes used in a more general way for a person who is in the process of Christian initiation.

**Christian Initiation:** The broad term for all of the processes in the congregation that welcome, form, and initiate persons into the life of the faith community. The term specifically refers to four stages and four services in a process related to the baptism of adults and the parallel processes for persons returning to the baptismal covenant and for the initiation of children.

***Catechist:*** The person the congregation called to be the guide of *catechumens*. The root word in this and other words that begin *"catech"* is the Greek word from which we get "echo." Today the catechist is a lay person who guides persons moving through the stages and services of Christian initiation.

***Catechesis:*** The instruction, primarily oral, used to form persons in the Christian faith and life. Catechesis encompasses all the forms, approaches, and methodologies used to form disciples. Catechesis aims at forming persons so that the Word of God resounds or echoes in them.

***Catechumen:*** The ancient Greek name for unbaptized adults preparing for initiation into the church through baptism, laying on of hands, and Holy Communion.

***Catechumenate:*** The ancient word for a basic structure and process related to forming and instructing adults preparing for baptism. The equivalent term is Christian initiation.

**Church Sponsors:** Persons from the congregation who join with parental sponsors as they prepare to present infants or children for baptism. When parents seeking to present a child for baptism are themselves inquirers, the sponsors may serve for both the parents and the children. (See **Parental Sponsor**.)

***Exorcisms:*** Public prayers for persons during the final stages of the catechumenate. Minor exorcisms took place during the *catechumenate* (formation stage), and major exorcisms took place during the intensive preparation stage.

**The Faithful:** A collective term for baptized Christians who live as disciples, keep their baptismal promises in communion with the church, and remain open to deeper conversion.

**Formation:** The process of structuring the Christian life. Formation, more than an intellectual grasp of Christian teaching, molds and shapes in Christ all of a person's being and doing. The basic elements of formation are worship, prayer, reflection on Scripture (and the core of Christian tradition), and ministry in daily life.

**Formational Groups**: Small groups guided by the catechist. The groups include people moving through the various stages of initiation and their sponsors. The groups may form in the inquiry stage and continue through the end of the process. Formational groups support those seeking God through learning to use the means of grace.

**Godparent**: The role of godparents is similar to that of sponsors, except that the godparents' role is a lifelong spiritual relationship with the candidate; they serve as faithful encouragers and guides from baptism onward. A godparent may or may not be a member of the denomination or the local congregation. Candidates may have both a sponsor and a godparent. Godparents are, however, to be active and committed Christians in the faith community where they hold membership.

**Hearer:** A person who has been welcomed into the community to hear the Word of God and who is in the process of formation following the initial stage of inquiry.

**Inquirer:** An inquirer is a person in the first stage of the catechumenal process. Inquirers are persons drawn to Christ and the life the church.

**Lectionary:** A lectionary is a table of Scripture readings that follows the calendar of the Christian year and serves as a resource for planning worship and preaching.

**Mystagogy:** The fourth and final stage in the catechumenal process, usually between Easter and Pentecost. In ancient practice, the newly baptized (neophytes) were instructed in the mystery of the sacraments that they had experienced and in the new life of faith and service they had begun.

**Neophyte:** The newly baptized Christian.

**Parental Sponsors:** When parents seek baptism for their children, they are designated parental sponsors, if they are baptized and professing members of the congregation. When parents are themselves inquirers or candidates for baptism or when they are returning to the baptismal covenant, this term does not apply.

**Paschal Mystery:** The paschal mystery is the heart of the Christian gospel: the passion, death, and resurrection of Jesus Christ. In it, Christians celebrate the central memory of their faith—their passage from sin and death to righteousness and life in Jesus Christ.

**Penitents:** Christians who sought to return to the Church after living a time outside the baptismal covenant. Penitents are referred to as returning members.

**Presentations:** Public occasions during the intensive formation stage in which candidates are presented with the Apostles' Creed and the Lord's Prayer. The presentations are not so much the distribution of information as they are a handing over of the traditions of the church—the imparting and entrusting of the central teaching and practice of the Christian faith and life.

**Returning Member:** When a person has been baptized, subsequently lived outside the communion of the church, and now desires to live as a professing member, he or she is a returning member. Returning members may fall into three general groupings: 1) those baptized as children, but never formed as disciples and integrated into the life of the community of faith; 2) those baptized and minimally formed in discipleship who have drifted away from the church; and 3) those baptized and formed as disciples, who have professed the Christian faith, and have chosen to depart from the baptismal covenant.

**Seeker:** A person who is on a quest for God or spiritual experience and knowledge. The term refers more to a state of the heart of a person than it does to a person in a particular stage related to baptism.

**Scrutinies:** This term refers to a public occasion of purification during the intensive preparation stage. The candidates faced the reality of evil and were delivered from it by the grace and power of God.

**Stages:** The progressive phases of conversion leading toward and following baptism.

**Inquiry Stage:** The first stage, of variable length, but sufficient to allow each inquirer opportunity to determine that he or she desires to become a Christian. This stage ends with a service of welcome in which inquirers become hearers.

**Formation Stage:** The second stage (also of variable length) in which "hearers" experience deeper levels of conversion and growing discernment of God's action in their daily life through worship, prayer, reflection on Scripture, and ministry. The stage ends with a service of calling hearers to baptism. Once called to baptism, hearers become candidates for baptism.

**Intensive Preparation Stage:** The third stage (of determined length—the weeks of Lent or the weeks of Advent-Christmas) in which candidates for baptism undergo intensive preparation for baptism. This stage includes examination of conscience and prayers for transformation, handing over The Lord's Prayer and The Apostles' Creed. This stage ends with baptism, laying on of hands and Eucharist.

**Integration Stage:** The fourth stage (of determined length—the weeks between Easter and Pentecost or between the Baptism of the Lord and Transfiguration Sunday) in which the newly baptized reflect on the life and mission of the church and on the mystery of the living Lord who encounters the church in the sacraments and the other means of grace. This stage ends with affirmation of ministry on Pentecost or the Transfiguration of the Lord.

**Sponsor:** Persons who walk with others during the stages of Christian initiation. For adults preparing for baptism or reaffirmation of baptism, sponsors know or get to know them so well that they can vouch for the conversion and sincere intention of each to live as a disciple of Christ.

## APPENDIX 1
## FORMATIONAL GROUP SESSIONS

This outline[75] suggests an approach for formational group sessions. The outline is adaptable and can be developed creatively to give it variety and appropriateness to the needs of those making the journey of Christian initiation. The assumption is that both those seeking God and their sponsors are active participants in the sessions. This outline can be used during any of the stages of Christian initiation. Generally, a catechist will lead the sessions.

The primary benefit of the experience-reflection approach is that it focuses the attention of the participants on listening to God in light of Scripture. (See pp. 60-61.)

**Open Bible Study Approach**

1. Attend worship with the entire congregation.

2. Gather for the weekly session of the formational group. The formational group may meet during worship (after the sermon), following worship, or on another day of the week.

3. Open with prayer, which may include an appropriate prayer from the hymnal, the Book of Worship, or another source.

4. Have one of the participants read slowly and deliberately one of the readings used in the service of worship. Generally, the gospel reading is preferred since the focus of the initiation process is on learning to be Jesus' disciples. Invite the hearers, inquirers, or candidates to listen for the words or phrases that stand out for them or speak most strongly to them.

5. Allow one minute of silence.

6. Invite everyone to say the word or phrase that touched him or her or held his or her attention.

7. Have another participant read the same Scripture passage again.

8. Tell the group you will now give them three to five minutes of silence to sit with the text. (When first starting this approach, three minutes will be sufficient. As the group progresses, five minutes will be better.) Give the group the time you said you would give them.

9. Invite the hearers to write and reflect on the questions: What do you hear in your heart? Where does this passage and *today's/this week's* sermon touch your life today?

10. Ask the participants to form groups of four to six people to talk about their experiences. Instruct the groups to speak from their experiences, using the pronoun I (I feel . . . I am . . . I think . . .). Be clear with the groups that this

is not a time to preach or teach or discuss or solve problems. Urge them to tell their own experiences.

11.  For a third time, read the same Scripture text again. (This is the third time for all to hear it during this session.)

12.  Invite silent reflection on the following: "From what you have heard and talked about, what does God want you to do or to be this week? How does God invite you to change?" Be concrete and specific. Another approach: "What do you take home with you this week?"

13.  Invite the participants to stay in the same small groups to talk about the questions.

14.  Let each person pray for the person on his or her right (naming what was just discussed). Ask participants to pray daily for the one they prayed for, until the group meets again.

15.  Gather the larger group to

  ◀ give instruction prepared ahead of time on questions and issues that have surfaced prior to the session or on a theme raised by the lectionary or the liturgical year

  ◀ close with prayer.

16.  Make announcements (if there are any to make) and give the group the readings for the next week.

17.  Close with song, prayer, or another action that is appropriate for departure to love and serve God and neighbor.

One way to vary this approach is to use the following questions for reflection times:

  ◀ after the first reading, "What does this reading say to you about God?"

  ◀ after the second reading, "What does this reading say to you about who you are?"

  ◀ after the third reading, "What do you hear God asking you to do or be this week?"

## APPENDIX 2
## HOLY COMMUNION AND THE UNBAPTIZED

There are good reasons to excuse inquirers, hearers, and candidates from the service following the congregation's prayers for them. The first two are practical considerations. Hearing the Scripture read and preached followed immediately by the gathering of the sponsors and inquirers, hearers, or candidates more closely links the experience of hearing the Word of God with reflection upon it. And in a culture of crowded schedules, holding the formational group on the same morning as worship may best accommodate the schedules of the hearers and their sponsors.

A pastoral and ecclesial consideration has to do with the order of the sacraments. *By Water and the Spirit* states: "Through baptism, persons are initiated into the Church; by the Lord's Supper, the Church is sustained by the life of faith. The Services of the Baptismal Covenant appropriately conclude with Holy Communion, through which the union of the new member with the Body of Christ is most fully expressed."[76] Since Holy Communion fully expresses the union of the new member with the Body of Christ, it can be argued that partaking of the holy meal should be reserved until after baptism.[77]

This is a particularly difficult issue for United Methodists, as we reclaim the sacramental and evangelical balance of our Wesleyan understandings of baptism. Honoring the classical order of the sacraments while holding to our Wesleyan experience that the Lord's Supper can be "an occasion for the reception of converting, justifying, and sanctifying grace" (*By Water and the Spirit*, p. 20) creates an awkward tension that is beyond the scope of this resource. Until General Conference speaks with clarity on this matter, United Methodist pastors and congregations will have to prayerfully exercise pastoral discernment and direction.

When the pastor and congregation are convinced that the order of initiation leading to communion with the church is a matter of sacramental integrity, the pastor should guide unbaptized inquirers, hearers and candidates in deciding whether or not to abstain from the holy meal until they are baptized.

# ENDNOTES

1   Adapted from Clifford Self's, *On the Lighter Side: God's Word Alive in Everyday Humor* (Palm Springs, FL: Sunday Publications, 1977), pp. 9-10

2   Among the staff of The General Board of Discipleship, we describe this essential ministry as the congregation's primary task or core process. We state the primary task as

   • *reaching out and receiving people into the congregation;*

   • *creating settings where their search for God is discovered and realized in Christ;*

   • *nurturing them in the Christian faith and equipping them for lives of discipleship;*

   • *sending them out to live as God's people—extending the church by loving God and neighbor in daily life so the world is more just and loving.*

   See Ezra Earl Jones, *Quest for Quality in the Church: A New Paradigm* (Nashville: Discipleship Resources, 1994), p. 32. This statement of primary task expresses the essential ministry of the congregation in a holistic way. The primary task is the core of what the congregation must do to serve people and to be faithful in its ministry in the world. Understand that the primary task is a functional statement. The Holy Spirit is the initiator for this ongoing process of ministry and for the making and sustaining of disciples. Without this linkage, the statement turns into something the people do for God rather than something the people do in and by the grace of God.

3   You may want to argue that the source goes back much further than the early church. To be sure, the creation and the promises to Abraham (Genesis 12:1-2) resound with the mission of God. This text from the Acts of the Apostles is used here because it reveals the embryonic expression of the essential ministry of the faith community and because the image of journey is useful for the way Christian initiation will be developed in this book.

4   See Robert E. Webber, *Liturgical Evangelism* (Ridgefield, Conn.: Morehouse Publishing House, 1992) for a brief treatment of the early church's way of evangelism. Webber's book cites many early sources and presents the recovery of this process in the twentieth century.

5   The ministry of the baptized in daily life is basic to Christian initiation as presented in this book. Daily life ministry will be more fully explored in Chapter Five.

6   Covenants are relationships between two parties. In baptism, God enters into covenant with us by claiming us for a life of grace in Christ. This action on God's part calls for a response from our side by which we accept God's call and grace making promises of faith and love. (See *The United Methodist Hymnal*, p. 32, for further reference to the phrase, "baptismal covenant.")

7   *The United Methodist Hymnal* (Nashville: The United Methodist Publishing House, 1989), p. 35, number 8; see also numbers 11 and 16. Copyright © 1989 by The United Methodist Publishing House. Reprinted by permission.

8   Loren B. Mead, *The Once and Future Church: Reinventing the Congregation for a New Mission Frontier* (Alban Institute, 1991), p. 50.

9   See Craig Kennet Miller, *Baby Boomer Spirituality* (Nashville: Discipleship Resources, 1993), pp. 95-96. While polls indicate that eighty percent of Americans believe the Bible is the Word of God, only forty percent indicate that they would turn to it first to test their religious beliefs. This does not mean that Americans, including Boomers and people of subsequent generations, are hostile or indifferent to the gospel. It does mean that churches cannot assume that seekers or church members know the basic beliefs of the Christian faith or the Bible or have any concept of the disciplines and the ways of Christian practice.

10  Aidan Kavanaugh, "Catechesis: Formation in Stages" in *The Baptismal Mystery and the Catechumenate*, ed. Michael W. Merriman (New York: The Church Hymnal Corporation, 1990), p. 37

11  *By Water and the Spirit: A United Methodist Understanding of Baptism* (Nashville: The General Board of Discipleship, 1996), p. 13.

12  See *By Water and the Spirit*, p. 7.

13  Kavanagh, *The Baptismal Mystery and the Catechumenate*, p. 38.

14  Kavanagh, *The Baptismal Mystery and the Catechumenate*, p. 37.

15  *The United Methodist Hymnal.* Copyright © 1989 by The United Methodist Publishing House. Reprinted by permission.

16  The biblical texts related to baptism are numerous and deserve careful study. Our purpose here is to make clear the roots of baptism in Scripture. In addition to Scripture, United Methodist doctrinal standards affirm God's action in baptism. See *The United Methodist Book of Discipline, 1992,* "The Articles of Religion of the Methodist Church" (pp. 62-63) and "The Confession of Faith of the Evangelical United Brethren" (p. 67). For a recent statement of our understanding of baptism, see *By Water and the Spirit: A United Methodist Understanding of Baptism,* which was adopted as an official interpretive statement on baptism by the 1996 General Conference of the United Methodist Church.

17  See *By Water and the Spirit*, pp. 1-4.

18  For further exploration of this reexamination, see the following: *Baptism, Eucharist and Ministry* (Geneva: The World Council of Churches, 1982); *By Water and the Spirit; This Gift of Water: The Practice and Theology of Baptism Among Methodists in America,* by Gayle Carlton Felton; *Baptism: Christ's Act in the Church,* by Laurence Hull Stookey (Nashville: Abingdon, 1982). For a more popularly written reappraisal of baptism, read William Willimon's *Remember Who You Are: Baptism, a Model for Christian Life* (Nashville: The Upper Room, 1980).

19 John Wesley took Christian antiquity as a decisive guideline in theology and ethics. Throughout his writings, early and late, he found in the ancient Christian writers a gold mine for the interpretation of Scripture. In his introduction to his collected works he listed his doctrinal norms as "Scripture, reason, and *Christian antiquity.*" See *The Works of John Wesley: Volume 1—Sermons I: 1-33,* edited by Albert C. Outler (Nashville: Abingdon Press, 1994), p. 324, footnote 47.

20 *Early Christian Baptism and the Catechumenate: West and East Syria,* ed. Thomas M. Finn (Collegeville, Minn.: The Liturgical Press, 1992), p. 86. Used with permission. Italics for emphasis.

21 Parker J. Palmer, *To Know as We Are Known: Education as a Spiritual Journey* (New York: Harper Collins Publishers, 1993). Palmer's critique of modern epistemology and pedagogy is extremely helpful. More helpful is his vision and recovery of the Christian spiritual tradition of knowing as journey and troth, which has a direct bearing on the approach this resource takes to Christian initiation.

22 As quoted in *Baptism,* by Martin E. Marty (Philadelphia: Fortress Press, 1962), p. 53.

23 Gayle Carlton Felton, *This Gift of Water, p. 178.* Copyright © by Abingdon Press. Reprinted by permission. Italics for emphasis.

24 From *The United Methodist Hymnal,* p. 37, section 11. Copyright © 1989 by The United Methodist Publishing House. Reprinted by permission.

25 If there are persons who are already baptized, they are called to continuing conversion, rather than baptism. See Part Two, "Services for Persons Returning to the Baptismal Covenant."

26 Persons already baptized (returning members) affirm the baptismal covenant with the confirming action of the church. Actions and symbols included are these: Call to remember baptism. Laying on of hands/anointing. Eucharist. Again, see Part Two, "Services for Persons Returning to the Baptismal Covenant."

27 I once heard a North American Christian tell of being in a Communion service in Korea. Though she did not understand the Korean language, she did understand what was happening because the ritual actions (lifting, blessing, breaking, and sharing the bread and cup) were familiar through repetition in her English language congregations at home.

28 The following list is based on the "Introduction" (81-85) to the services of the baptismal covenant in *The United Methodist Book of Worship* (1992), which is an official statement adopted by The General Conference. 1)avoid indiscriminate baptism 2) provide needed instruction and support 3) enact corporate sponsorship by the congregation as a whole 4) allow for unusual circumstances when persons cannot be present in congregational worship 5) affirm that God's prevenient grace is available and sufficient for children who face imminent death 6) affirm further steps and growth in faith with ritual celebration within the baptismal covenant 7) do not administer baptism for any person more than once 8) prepare those who were not old enough to take vows for themselves to make their personal profession of faith in a service called confirmation 9) encourage reaffirmation of the baptismal covenant at significant moments for individuals, such as transfer of membership, after a time of lapse in discipleship, or following significant steps in their personal faith journey 10) do not use water in ways that can be interpreted as baptism when confirming or reaffirming faith. This section in the *UMBOW* merits careful study and reflection by pastors and catechists. In addition, see *By Water and the Spirit: A United Methodist Understanding of Baptism.*

29 This expression comes from a talk on the catechumenal process given by the Reverend Mark MacDonald in November 1993 at Lake Oswego, Oregon.

30 *Church Membership Initiative: Narrative Summary of Findings/Research Summary Findings,* 1993. (Aid Association for Lutherans, 4321 North Ballard Road, Appleton, WI, 54919-0001), p. 6.

31 The Christian initiation of adults has been revived in a number of denominations in the last half of the twentieth century. The Roman Catholic Church called for its restoration in *The Constitution on the Sacred Liturgy,* and introduced the *Rite of Christian Initiation of Adults* in 1974. More recently, the Protestant Episcopal Church in the U. S. in its *Book of Occasional Services 1991* has made provision for the catechumenal process. The Evangelical Lutheran Church in Canada has also developed resources for Christian initiation, entitled *Living Witnesses.* The Mennonites have produced a resource entitled *Welcoming New Christians: A Guide for the Christian Initiation of Adults.*

32 For a look at nine of these churches, see *Church for the Unchurched,* by George G. Hunter III (Nashville: Abingdon, 1996).

33 Eugene H. Peterson, *The Contemplative Pastor* (Grand Rapids: William B. Eerdmans Publishing Co., 1989), p. 115. Reprinted by permission.

34 Peterson, p. 116.

35 See David Lowes Watson, *Forming Christian Disciples: The Role of Covenant Discipleship and Class Leaders in the Congregation* (Nashville: Discipleship Resources, 1991). The discussion in Part I of Watson's book offers solid conceptual insight to the coming reign of God and Jesus' call to discipleship that is "inside out."

36 Words and music copyright © Hope Publishing Company, 380 S. Main Place, Carol Stream IL 60188. Used with permission.

37 Other resources in *The Christian Initiation Series* will provide you and your congregation with needed information and support for implementing the ministries of welcoming, forming, and initiating people into the community of faith. Contact The General Board of Discipleship, (P.O. Box 840, Nashville, TN 37202) for additional information about the series.

38 This expression is used in *Guiding Your Parish Through the Christian Initiation Process: A Handbook for Leaders,* by William R. Bruns (Cincinnati: St. Anthony Messenger Press, 1993), p. 12.

39 The General Board of Discipleship's Congregational Leaders Team will assist you in locating a congregation that is already living out the Christian initiation process in its daily life together. (Contact The General Board of Discipleship, PO Box 840, Nashville TN 37202; 615/340-7070)

40 There are different meanings of experience. I am not using the term experience in the same sense as that used by John Dewey. As the father of American education, he understood that the whole educational enterprise was based on experience. For Dewey, Hegel, and others, experience was a category to be naturalistically defined and refined through scientific methods of rational and empirical research. By contrast, I am calling for something far more modest and, at the same time, more in keeping with the classical wisdom of the Patristic period—not a definition or concept of experience *per se*, but a simple way of growing in faith through openness to God in basic relationships and spiritual disciplines. This is what Wesley meant by "experimental" and practical divinity.

41 As cited in Thomas M. Finn's *Early Christian Baptism and the Catechumenate: West and East Syria*. (Collegeville, Minn. The Liturgical Press, pp. 43-44.

42 See Theodore Jennings, *Good News to the Poor* (Nashville: Abingdon, 1992).

43 The story of the Bible is a story in *time*. The biblical story is full of references to God's action in time. Genesis 1, tells of what God created on the first *day*, the second, and so on. From the beginning, the Sabbath, the seventh day, is hallowed as a day when God rested. In Exodus, the Lord said to the people, "Remember this day on which you came out of Egypt, out of the house of slavery" (Exodus 13:3). The Passover was set to be celebrated in "the first month, on the fourteenth day of the month, at twilight" (Leviticus 23:5). The connection of the people to God, and the rehearsal of their identity, was tied to a calendar of faithful observance and ritual.

The early Christian community in Jerusalem was shaped in worship using the Jewish calendar, but with new meaning rooted in Jesus' death, resurrection, ascension, and the outpouring of the Spirit. Passover was the setting for what we know as the Lord's Supper, and Jesus' death pointed to a new Passover lamb who takes away the sin of the world. The Day of Pentecost was the occasion for the outpouring of the Spirit as the power that impelled the new community to be witnesses beginning in Jerusalem to the ends of the earth.

Jesus' resurrection on the first day of the week introduced a radical recalculation of time! The first day of the week became the eighth day of creation: the day of God making all things new. Jesus, by virtue of the resurrection, was called the "firstborn of all creation . . . the beginning, the firstborn from the dead" (Colossians 1:15, 18). Sunday, the first day of the week, was marked as the day of encounter with the risen Lord by the sharing of a meal, the breaking of bread. According to Luke, the risen Lord was made known to the disciples on that first day (Luke 24:30-43). In Acts, Luke writes, "On the first day of the week, when we met to break bread. . . ." (Acts 20:7). There are clear connections of the Lord's Day with baptism and the Eucharist. In John's Gospel the narrative recalls numerous meetings of the risen Lord and his followers: with Mary in the morning, with the disciples (except for Thomas) in the evening, with the eleven one week later.

Easter and Sunday stand at the heart of the church's keeping time with Christ. Easter and the events of what we now call Holy Week are the cornerstone of the Christian year. The first day of the week becomes a little Easter at the head of every week. All time finds its orientation in the resurrection of our Lord. Memory looks back to the dawn that marked the beginning of God's new creation. Faith and hope look forward to the completion of God's new creation when all who have been united with Christ in a death like his through baptism will be made alive in a resurrection like his (Romans 6:3-11) and the last enemy, death, will be destroyed (1 Corinthians 15:26).

44 For more details on the calendar of the Christian year, see *The New Handbook of the Christian Year*, Hoyt Hickman, et. al. (Nashville: Abingdon, 1992), pp. 13-25.

45 *The United Methodist Hymnal* p. 6. Copyright © 1989 by The United Methodist Publishing House. Reprinted with permission.

46 *Egeria: Diary of a Pilgrimage*, trans. George E. Gingras, Vol 38, *Ancient Christian Writers* (New York: Newman Press, 1968).

47 This very helpful summary of the emphases of worship through history comes from an introductory article written by Per Harling in *Worshipping Ecumenically* (Geneva: World Council of Churches, 1995), p. 5. Reprinted with permission.

48 See *Signs of Wonder*, by Robert Webber (Nashville: Abbott/Martyn, 1992).

49 Ron Lewinski, as cited in *Robert Hovda: The Amen Corner*, ed. John F. Baldovin (Collegeville, Minn.: Pueblo, 1994), p. 111.

50 A United Methodist version of the Revised Common Lectionary is published in *The United Methodist Book of Worship*, 227-237. The ecumenical version was developed by the Consultation on Common Texts and is published as *The Revised Common Lectionary* (Nashville: Abingdon, 1992).

51 *The United Methodist Book of Worship* (Nashville: The United Methodist Publishing House, 1992), 332-323.

52 For a fuller discussion of the lectionary texts for Lent, Holy Week, and the Great Fifty Days as a short course in the meaning of baptism, see *The New Prayerbook Guide for Christian Education*, edited and revised by Joseph P. Russell (Cambridge, Mass.: Cowley, 1996).

53 The Sixth Sunday in Lent, Passion/Palm Sunday, is also the beginning of Holy Week and begins the congregation's entry into the passion of Jesus.

54 See *The New Handbook of the Christian Year*, pp. 105-110. Also see the introductory material in *UMBOW* for Lent (320) and Easter (368).

55 Thomas M. Finn, *Early Christian Baptism and the Catechumenate: Italy, North Africa, and Egypt*. (Collegeville, Minn.: A Michael Glazier Book, 1992), p. 96.

56 See Henry H. Knight III, *The Presence of God in the Christian Life: John Wesley and the Means of Grace* (Metuchen, N.J.: The Scarecrow Press, Inc., 1992), pp. 122-126.

57 *Robert Hovda: The Amen Corner*, ed. John F. Baldovin (Collegeville, Minn.: The Liturgical Press, 1994), p. 111.

58 See *Faith-Sharing Congregations: Developing a Strategy for the Congregation as Evangelist*, by Roger K. Swanson and Shirley F. Clement (Nashville: Discipleship Resources, 1996). The authors explore the many facets of hospitality and welcome under three basic headings: welcoming ministries, belonging ministries, and discipling ministries.

59 Doug Murren and Mike Meeks, "How Your Church Can Evangelize," *Leadership* magazine (Summer 1995), p. 93.

60 In addition to the resources in UMBOW, see *The New Handbook of the Christian Year* for additional resources and options in preparing for this service.

61 To deepen and stretch your imagery of baptism and its connection to Easter, read and reflect on some of the early baptismal sermons of Theodore of Mopsuestia, Cyril of Jerusalem, Gregory of Nyssa, and others. See the material under the headings "Initiation: Joined to Christ and the Church," "Baptism and the Baptismal Covenant," and "The Church Gathers for Eucharist" in *Gracious Voices,* ed. William McDonald (Discipleship Resources, 1997). Also see *Early Christian Baptism and the Catechumenate* (Volume 5 in *Message of the Fathers of the Church*), Thomas M. Finn, ed.

62 Frederick P. Ludolph, *Living Witnesses: The Adult Catechumenate: Preparing Adults for Baptism and Ministry in the Church* (Evangelical Lutheran Church in Canada, 1992), p. 7.

63 From John Wesley's "The Nature, Design, and General Rules of Our Societies" which are still part of United Methodist doctrinal standards in *The United Methodist Book of Discipline,1992*, p. 71. Copyright © 1992 by The United Methodist Publishing House. Used by permission.

64 For additions to this list of the means of grace in the writings and work of John Wesley, see Henry H. Knight III's *The Presence of God in the Christian Life*, particularly Chapter V.

65 See *The United Methodist Book of Discipline,1992*, pp. 72-73.

66 Attributed to Aidan Kavanagh. John W. B. Hill, *Making Disciples: Serving Those Who Are Entering the Christian Life* (Toronto: The Hoskin Group, 1991), p. 92.

67 See *The United Methodist Hymnal*, p. 34.

68 See David Lowes Watson, *Covenant Discipleship: Christian Formation Through Mutual Accountability* (Nashville: Discipleship Resources, 1991), particularly Chapters 4 and 5.

69 The process of Christian initiation is most clearly related to the Lent-Easter-Pentecost cycle. This introduction and commentary refer only to that cycle. It can also be used in relationship to the Advent-Christmas-Transfiguration cycle. See the chart on page 43 in Chapter Three and pp. 82-83 in Chapter Six for adaptation to other seasons.

70 Reprinted from *Living Witnesses: The Adult Catechumenate—Congregational Prayers to Accompany the Catechumenl Process*, by Gordon Lathrop, p. 10, copyright © 1992 ELCIC, by permission of the Evangelical Lutheran Church in Canada.

71 For information about group resources that support and sustain disciples, contact The General Board of Discipleship, P. O. Box 840, Nashville TN 37202 (800-814-7833). The trilogy of books, *Forming Christian Disciples, Covenant Discipleship,* and *Class Leader,* by David Lowes Watson are strongly recommended as a basis for establishing a comprehensive system for making and sustaining disciples. There are related videos and other resources for Covenant Discipleship for youth (*We Are the Branches*) and for children (*Sprouts*).

72 From a text in *The Book of Alternative Services of the Anglican Church in Canada* (Toronto: Anglican Book Centre, 1985), p. 305. Copyright © 1985 by the General Synod of the Anglican Church of Canada. Reprinted with permission. The quoted Scripture text is from the New Revised Standard Version. The section beginning "He also taught" is from *Making Disciples,* by John W. Hill (Toronto: Hoskins Books on Worship, 1991), p. 47. Copyright " 1991, The Hoskins Group, Hoskins@niagara.com. Used with permission.

73 From *The United Methodist Book of Worship.* Copyright " 1992 by The United Methodist Publishing House. Reprinted by permission.

74 From *Making Disciples*, copyright © 1991, J. W. B. Hill, p. 48. Used with permission.

75 This outline is based on material in *The Catechumenal Process: Adult Initiation and Formation for Christian Life and Ministry*, p. 195 (New York: The Church Hymnal Corporation, 1990). "Appendix C" in *The Catechumenal Process* has a number of other resources for use in formational groups.

76 *By Water and the Spirit: A United Methodist Understanding of Baptism*, p. 20.

77 For further exploration of this issue within the Wesleyan historical context, see John C. Bowmer's *The Sacrament of the Lord's Supper in Early Methodism* (Dacre Press, 1951), chapter 8. See also Bowmer's article "A Converting Ordinance and the Open Table" published in the *Proceedings of the Wesley Historical Society*, Volume XXXIV, Part 5, March 1964.